THE

SHADOW OF THE ROCK,

AND

OTHER RELIGIOUS POEMS.

NEW AND ENLARGED EDITION.

NEW YORK:
ANSON D. F. RANDOLPH & CO.,
900 BROADWAY, COR. 20th ST.

EDWARD O. JENKINS,
PRINTER AND STEREOTYPER,
20 North William Street, N. Y.

ROBERT RUTTER,
BINDER,
94 Beekman Street, N. Y.

The first edition of this book was issued in 1865 as a companion-volume to the Changed Cross, and was received with great favor by the religious public. The present edition contains forty additional poems, selected from many sources. The names of the authors, so far as they could be ascertained, will be found in the index.

November, 1872.

THE Poems contained in this Volume have been selected from many sources, and, so far as known, the names of the authors appended. The publisher has designed it as a companion-book to THE CHANGED CROSS, which has proved so acceptable to a large class of Christian readers.

CONSIDER.

Consider
The lilies of the field whose bloom is brief
We are as they;
Like them we fade away,
As doth a leaf.

Consider
The sparrows of the air of small account;
Our God doth view
Whether they fall or mount—
He guards us too.

Consider
The lilies that do neither spin nor toil,
Yet are most fair;
What profits all this care
And all this toil?

Consider
The birds that have no barn nor harvest weeks
God gives them food;
Much more our Father seeks
To do us good.

THE

SHADOW OF THE ROCK

AND OTHER POEMS.

THE SHADOW OF THE ROCK.

THE Shadow of the Rock!
    Stay, Pilgrim, stay!
Night treads upon the heels of day;
There is no other resting-place this way.
        The Rock is near,
        The well is clear—
    Rest in the Shadow of the Rock!

The Shadow of the Rock!
    The desert wide
Lies round thee like a trackless tide,
In waves of sand forlornly multiplied.
        The sun is gone,
        Thou art alone—
    Rest in the Shadow of the Rock!

The Shadow of the Rock!
    All come alone;

All, ever since the sun hath shone,
Who traveled by this road have come alone.
Be of good cheer—
A home is here—
Rest in the Shadow of the Rock!

The Shadow of the Rock!
Night veils the land;
How the palms whisper as they stand!
How the well tinkles faintly through the sand!
Cool water take
Thy thirst to slake—
Rest in the Shadow of the Rock!

The Shadow of the Rock!
Abide! Abide!
This Rock moves ever at thy side,
Pausing to welcome thee at eventide.
Ages are laid
Beneath its shade—
Rest in the Shadow of the Rock!

The Shadow of the Rock!
Always at hand,
Unseen it cools the noon-tide land,
And quells the fire that flickers in the sand.
It comes in sight
Only at night—
Rest in the Shadow of the Rock!

The Shadow of the Rock!
'Mid skies storm-riven
It gathers shadows out of heaven,
And holds them o'er us all night cool and even.
Through the charmed air
Dew falls not there—
Rest in the Shadow of the Rock!

The Shadow of the Rock!
To angels' eyes
This Rock its shadow multiplies,
And at this hour in countless places lies.
One Rock, one shade,
O'er thousands laid—
Rest in the Shadow of the Rock!

The Shadow of the Rock!
To weary feet,
That have been diligent and fleet,
The sleep is deeper and the shade more sweet.
O weary, rest!
Thou art sore pressed—
Rest in the Shadow of the Rock!

The Shadow of the Rock!
Thy bed is made;
Crowds of tired souls like thine are laid
This night beneath the self-same placid shade.

They who rest here
Wake with Heaven near—
Rest in the Shadow of the Rock.

The Shadow of the Rock!
Pilgrim! sleep sound;
In night's swift hours with silent bound,
The Rock will put thee over leagues of ground,
Gaining more way
By night than day—
Rest in the Shadow of the Rock!

The Shadow of the Rock!
One day of pain,
Thou scarce wilt hope the Rock to gain,
Yet there wilt sleep thy last sleep on the plain
And only wake
In Heaven's daybreak—
Rest in the Shadow of the Rock!

NIGHT SONG.

HEART, be still!
In the darkness of thy woe,
Bow thee silently and low;
Comes to thee whate'er God will;—
Be thou still!

Be thou still!
Vainly all thy words are spoken;
Till the Word of God hath broken
Life's dark mysteries—good or ill—
Be thou still!

Sleep thou still!
'Tis thy Father's work of grace,
Wait thou yet before His face,
He'll thy sure deliverance will·
Keep thou still!

Lord my God!
By thy grace, O may I be
All-submission, silently,
To the chastenings of thy rod;
Lord my God!

Shepherd, King!
From thy fullness, grant to me
Still, yet fearless faith in Thee,
Till, from night the day shall spring!
Shepherd, King!

UPWARD!

UPWARD, where the stars are burning,
Silent, silent in their turning
Round the never-changing pole;
Upward, where the sky is brightest,
Upward, where the blue is lightest,
Lift I now my longing soul!

Far above that arch of gladness,
Far beyond those clouds of sadness,
Are the many mansions fair!
Far from pain, and sin, and folly,
In that palace of the holy,
I would find my mansion there!

Where the glory brightly dwelleth,
Where the new song sweetly swelleth,
And the discord never comes;
Where life's stream is ever laving,
And the palm is ever waving—
That must be the home of homes!

Where the Lamb on high is seated,
By ten thousand voices greeted,
Lord of lords and King of kings!

Son of man, they crown, they crown Him!
Son of God, they own, they own Him!
  With His name the palace rings!

Blessing, honor, without measure,
Heavenly riches, earthly treasure,
  Lay we at His blessèd feet!
Poor the praise that now we render;
Loud shall be our voices yonder,
  When before His Throne we meet

HE KNOWETH ALL.

THE twilight falls, the night is near,
  I fold my work away,
And kneel to One who bends to hear
  The story of the day.

The old, old story; yet I kneel
  To tell it at Thy call;
And cares grow lighter as I feel
  That Jesus knows them all.

Yes, all! The morning and the night,
  The joy, the grief, the loss,
The roughened path, the sunbeam bright,
  The hourly thorn and cross.

Thou knowest all—I lean my head,
  My weary eyelids close;
Content and glad awhile to tread
  This path, since Jesus knows!

And He has loved me! All my heart
  With answering love is stirred,
And every anguished pain and smart
  Finds healing in the Word.

So here I lay me down to rest,
  As nightly shadows fall,
And lean, confiding, on His breast,
  Who knows and pities all!

HOMEWARDS!

DROPPING down the troubled river,
  To the tranquil, tranquil shore;
Dropping down the misty river,
Time's willow-shaded river,
  To the spring-embosomed shore;
Where the sweet light shineth ever,
  And the sun goes down no more.
  O wondrous, wondrous shore!

Dropping down the winding river,
  To the wide and welcome sea;

Dropping down the narrow river,
Man's weary, wayward river,
  To the blue and ample sea;
Where no tempest wrecketh ever
  Where the sky is fair and free;
  O joyous, joyous sea!

Dropping down the noisy river,
  To our peaceful, peaceful home;
Dropping down the turbid river,
Earth's bustling, crowded river,
  To our gentle, gentle home;
Where the rough roar riseth never,
  And the vexings cannot come;
  O loved and longed for home!

Dropping down the eddying river,
  With a Helmsman true and tried
Dropping down the perilous river—
Mortality's dark river,
  With a sure and Heavenly Guide;
Even Him who, to deliver
  My soul from death, hath died;
  O Helmsman, true and tried!

Dropping down the rapid river,
  To the dear and deathless land;
Dropping down the well-known river,
Life's swoll'n and rushing river.

To the resurrection-land;
Where the living, live for ever,
And the dead have joined the band,
O fair and blessed land!

THE LOVING CUP.

COME, drink ye, drink ye, all, of it,
Pale children of a King;
No poison mingles in the draught,
So, while ye suffer, sing.
'Tis Love's own Life hath won it us,
Christ's lip hath pressed the brim,—
Come, drink ye, drink ye, all, of it,
In fellowship with Him!

O shun not thou the Loving Cup,
Nor tremble at its hue;
There is no bitter in the bowl,
But Jesus drank it, too.
He counts thy tears, and knows thy pain,
Yea, every woe is weighed;
And not a cross He bids thee bear,
But once on Him was laid.

Come, drink thou of the Loving Cup!
Thou wouldst not pass it by?
'Tis kept for every chosen one
Of God's dear family:

Nor, unbelieving, turn aside;
  The Lord the cup bestows;
And O His face, above thee bent,
  With love and pity glows!

Those hands, once bleeding on the Cross,
  Are now outstretched to bless;
He draws thee closer to His heart
  For that draught's bitterness;
He hears thy faintly-sobbing breath,
  He marks each quivering limb;
He drank a cup for thee alone—
  Child! drink it now with Him.

Let earth bring forth her bitter herbs,
  Soon all their power shall cease;
Come tribulation if it will,
  With Christ's abiding Peace.
I take the cup—the Loving Cup,
  Thrice blessèd shall it be;
I would not miss one gift, O Lord,
  Thy Blood hath bought for me!

THE SINNER'S FRIEND.

O THOU, the contrite sinner's Friend,
Who loving, lov'st them to the end,
On this alone my hopes depend,
  That Thou wilt plead for me!

When, weary in the Christian race,
Far-off appears my resting-place,
And fainting, I mistrust Thy grace—
Then, Saviour, plead for me!

When I have err'd and gone astray
Afar from Thine and Wisdom's way,
And see no glimmering guiding ray—
Still, Saviour, plead for me!

When Satan, by my sins made bold,
Strives from Thy cross to loose my hold
Then with Thy pitying arms enfold,
And plead, oh, plead for me!

And when my dying hour draws near,
Darken'd with anguish, guilt, and fear,
Then to my fainting sight appear,
Pleading in Heaven for me!

When the full light of Heavenly day
Reveals my sins in dread array,
Say, Thou hast wash'd them all away;
Oh, say, Thou plead'st for me!

THE WAY IS LONG AND DREARY

THE way is long and dreary,
The path is bleak and bare;
Our feet are worn and weary,
But we will not despair.
More heavy was Thy burthen,
More desolate Thy way;
O Lamb of God, who takest
The sin of the world away,
Have mercy on us!

The snows lie thick around us,
In the dark and gloomy night;
And the tempest wails above us,
And the stars have hid their light.
But blacker was the darkness
Round Calvary's Cross that day.
O Lamb of God, that takest
The sin of the world away,
Have mercy on us!

Our hearts are faint with sorrow,
Heavy and sad to bear;
For we dread the bitter morrow,
But we will not despair.

Thou knowest all our anguish,
  And Thou wilt bid it cease.
O Lamb of God! who takest
  The sin of the world away,
    Give us Thy peace!

THE DEATH OF A BELIEVER

THE Apostle slept; a light shone in the prison
    An angel touched his side;
"Arise," he said, and quickly he hath risen,
    His fettered arms untied.

The watchers saw no light at midnight gleaming
    They heard no sound of feet;
The gates fly open, and the saint still dreaming,
    Stands free upon the street.

So when the Christian's eyelid droops and closes
    In Nature's parting strife,
A friendly angel stands where he reposes
    To wake him up to life.

He gives a gentle blow, and so releases
    The spirit from its clay;
From sin's temptations and from life's distresses
    He bids it come away.

It rises up, and from its darksome mansion
It takes its silent flight,
And feels its freedom in the large expansion
Of Heavenly air and light.

Behind, it hears Time's iron gates close faintly;
It is now far from them,
For it has reached the city of the saintly,
The new Jerusalem!

A voice is heard on earth of kinsfolk weeping
The loss of one they love;
But he is gone where the redeemed are keeping
A festival above.

The mourners throng the way, and from the steeple
The funeral-bell tolls slow;
But on the golden streets the holy people
Are passing to and fro;

And saying, as they meet, "Rejoice! another
Long-waited-for is come;
The Saviour's heart is glad, a younger brother
Hath reached the Father's home!"

EARTH AND HEAVEN

THE roseate hues of early dawn,
  The brightness of the day;
The crimson of the sunset sky,
  How fast they fade away!
Oh, for the pearly gates of Heaven!
  Oh, for the golden floor!
Oh, for the Sun of Righteousness,
  That setteth nevermore!

The brightest hopes we cherish here
  How fast they tire and faint;
How many a spot defiles the robe
  That wraps an earthly saint!
Oh, for a heart that never sins!
  Oh, for a soul wash'd white!
Oh, for a voice to praise our King,
  Nor weary, day nor night!

Here faith is ours, and Heavenly hope,
  And grace to lead us higher;
But there are perfectness, and peace,
  Beyond our best desire.
Oh, by Thy love, and anguish, Lord,
  And by Thy life laid down,
Grant that we fall not from Thy grace,
  Nor cast away our crown!

UNDERTAKE FOR ME!

AS those that watch for the day,
  Through the restless night of pain,
When the first faint streaks of gray
  Bring rest and ease again—
As they turn their sleepless eyes
  The Eastern sky to see,
Long hours before sunrise—
  So waiteth my soul for Thee!

As those that watch for the day,
  Through the long, long night of grief,
When the soul can only pray
  That the day may bring relief,—
When the eyes, with weeping spent,
  No dawn of hope can see,
But the heart keeps watch intent,—
  So waiteth my soul for Thee!

As those that watch for the day,
  Through that deepest night of all,
When trembling, and sin have sway,
  And the shades of Thy absence fall;
As they search through clouds of fear
  The Morning Star to see,
And the Light of Life appear—
  So waiteth my soul for Thee!

As those that watch for the day,
  And know that the day will rise,
Though the weary hours delay,
  As they pass under midnight skies,
Though the Sun of Righteousness
  Only Faith's eye can see,
Because Thou hast promised to bless—
  Lord Jesus, I wait for Thee!

THE UNDISCOVERED COUNTRY.

COULD we but know
  The land that ends our dark, uncertain travel
Where lie those happier hills and meadows low
Ah! if beyond the spirit's inmost cavil
  Aught of that country could we surely know,
    Who would not go?

Might we but hear
The hovering angels' high imagined chorus,
  Or catch, betimes, with wakeful eyes and clear
One radiant vista of the realm before us—
  With one rapt moment given to see and hear,
    Ah, who would fear?

Were we quite sure
To find the peerless friend who left us lonely,
  Or there, by some celestial stream as pure,

To gaze in eyes that here were lovelit only—
This weary mortal coil, were we quite sure,
Who would endure ?

THE ANSWER.

"WHO would not go"
With buoyant steps, to gain that blessèd portal,
Which opens to the land we long to know ?
Where shall be satisfied the soul's immortal,
Where we shall drop the wearying and the wo
In resting so ?

"Ah, who would fear ?"
Since, sometimes through the distant pearly portal,
Unclosing to some happy soul a-near,
We catch a gleam of glorious light immortal,
And strains of heavenly music faintly hear,
Breathing good cheer !

"Who would endure"
To walk in doubt and darkness with misgiving,
When He whose tender promises are sure—
The Crucified, the Lord, the Ever-living—
Keeps us those "mansions" evermore secure
By waters pure ?

Oh, wondrous land!
Fairer than all our spirit's fairest dreaming:
"Eye hath not seen"—no heart can understand
The things prepared, the cloudless radiance streaming.
How longingly we wait our Lord's command—
His opening hand!

Oh, dear ones there!
Whose voices, hushed, have left our pathway lonely,
We come, ere long, your blessèd home to share;
We take the guiding Hand, we trust it only—
Seeing, by faith, beyond this clouded air,
That land so fair!

LORD, ARE THERE FEW THAT BE SAVED?

WHETHER there many be, or few,
Elect the heavenly goal to win,
Truly, I know not—this I know—
That none who march with footsteps slow,
That none who fight with hearts untrue,
That none who serve with service cold,
The Eternal City can behold,
Or enter in.

Whether there many be who thrive
  In their vast suit for that vast love,
Truly, I know not—this I know—
That love lives not in outward show;
That but to seek is not to strive;
That thankless praises, empty prayers,
Can claim no bond, for will of theirs
      His court to move.

How long the door, unfastened now,
  Shall open by His grace remain,
Truly, I know not—this I know—
If once that grace aside He throw,
No tear, no sigh, no anguished vow,
Gnashing of teeth, wringing of hands,
Shall draw the bolts and loose the bands
      Ever again.

How long His wrath may yet forbear,
  And sheathe His sword, and hide His rod,
Truly, I know not—this I know—
He points the arrows of His bow,
While speed apace that night of fear,
Of debt unpaid, of work undone,
Where Mercy, Pardon, Hope is none,
      Laid up with God!

LORD, THOU ART MINE!

LORD, Thou art mine,
Send help to me!
Christ, I am Thine,
Deliver me!
Then shall I praise and sing,
"My soul, bless thou thy God and King!"

Mercies are Thine,
Remember me!
Sad sins are mine,
Oh, pardon me!
Then shall I praise and sing,
"My soul, bless thou thy God and King!"

Goodness is Thine,
Lord, pity me!
Evil is mine,
Forsake not me!
Then shall I praise and sing,
"My soul, bless thou thy God and King!"

All light is Thine,
Oh, shine on me!
Darkness is mine,
Enlighten me!
Then shall I praise and sing,
"My soul, bless thou thy God and King!"

True life is Thine,
Breathe it on me!
All death is mine,
Oh, quicken me!
Then shall I praise and sing,
"My soul, bless thou thy God and King!"

WE STOOD BESIDE THE RIVER

WE stood beside the river,
Whence all our souls must go,
Bearing a loved one in our arms,
Our hearts repeating the alarms
That came across the river;
And saw the sun decline in mist,
That rose until her brow it kissed,
And left it cold as snow.

Watching beside the river,
With every ebb and flow,
Fond hopes within our hearts would spring,
Until another warning ring
Came o'er the fearful river.
We saw the flush, the brightness fade,
The loving lips look grieved and sad,
The white hands whiter grow.

Watching by the river,
With anguish none can tell·

And trembling hearts and hands, we strove
To save the darling of our love
From going down the river!
Oh, powerless, but to weep and pray,
And grieve for one who, far away,
Had said his last farewell!

Weeping by the river,
There came a blessèd time,
A solemn calm spread all around,
Making it seem like holy ground,
Beside the silent river!
The world receding from our eyes,
Caught gleams of that dear land which lies
In Canaan's happy clime!

And there, beside the river,
Came lessons strange and sweet,
The perfect work of patience done,
The warfare finished, victory won
With weak hands by the river!
The childlike fear, the clinging love,
The darkness brightened from above,
The peace at Jesus' feet!

Waiting by the river,
Through mingled night and day,
Sweet memories round our hearts we bring,
Of Jesus' love and Heaven we sing,

To soothe her by the river;
And wept for one whose heart would break,
Be pitiful for Jesus' sake.
Father in heaven, we pray!

Standing by the river,
We closed the weary eyes,
In Jesus' arms we laid her down,
A lovely jewel for His crown.
He bore her through the river,
And clothed her in a robe so white,
Too beautiful for mortal sight,
And took her to the skies!

KNEELING AT THE THRESHOLD.

I'M kneeling at the threshold, weary, faint, and sore;
Waiting for the dawning, for the opening of the door;
Waiting till the Master shall bid me rise and come,
To the glory of His presence, to the gladness of His home!

A weary path I've traveled, 'mid darkness, storm, and strife:
Bearing many a burden, struggling for my life;

But now the morn is breaking, my toil will soon
be o'er,
I'm kneeling at the threshold, my hand is on the
door

Methinks I hear the voices of the blessèd as they
stand,
Singing in the sunshine in the far-off sinless land;
Oh, would that I were with them, amid their shin
ing throng,
Mingling in their worship, joining in their song!

The friends that started with me have entered
long ago;
One by one they left me struggling with the foe;
Their pilgrimage was shorter, their triumph surer
won,
How lovingly they'll hail me, when all my toil is
done!

With them the blessèd angels that know no grief
or sin,
I see them by the portals, prepared to let me in.
O Lord, I wait Thy pleasure; Thy time and way
are best;
But I'm wasted, worn, and weary; O Father, bid
me rest!

LEAVE GOD TO ORDER ALL THY WAYS.

LEAVE God to order all thy ways,
And hope in Him, whate'er betide;
Thou'lt find Him in the evil days
An all-sufficient strength and guide.
Who trusts in God's unchanging love,
Builds on the rock that naught can move.

What can these anxious cares avail—
These never-ceasing moans and sighs?
What can it help us to bewail
Each painful moment as it flies?
Our cross and trials do but press
The heavier for our bitterness.

Only your restless heart keep still,
And wait in cheerful hope, content
To take whate'er His gracious will,
His all-discerning love, hath sent;
Nor doubt our inmost wants are known
To Him who chose us for His own!

He knows when joyful hours are best,
He sends them as He sees it meet;
When thou hast borne its fiery test,
And now art freed from all deceit,
He comes to thee all unaware.
And makes thee own His loving care.

Nor, in the heat of pain and strife,
  Think God hath cast thee off unheard
Nor that the man whose prosperous life
  Thou enviest, is of him preferred.
Time passes, and much change doth bring
And sets a bound to everything.

All are alike before His face:
  'Tis easy to our God most high
To make the rich man poor and base,
  To give the poor man wealth and joy.
True wonders still of Him are wrought,
Who setteth up and brings to naught!

Sing, pray, and swerve not from His ways,
  But do thine own part faithfully;
Trust His rich promises of grace,
  So shall it be fulfilled in thee:
God never yet forsook at need
The soul that trusted Him indeed!

WE GLORY IN TRIBULATION ALSO.

"WITHIN this leaf, to every eye
  So little worth, doth hidden lie
Most rare and subtile fragrancy.
Wouldst thou its secret strength unbind?
Crush it, and thou shalt perfume find
Sweet as Arabia's spicy wind.

"In this dull stone so poor, and bare
Of shape or luster, patient care
Will find for thee a jewel rare!
But first must skillful hands essay,
With file and flint, to clear away
The film which hides its fire from day.

'This leaf! This stone! It is thy heart;
It must be crushed by pain and smart;
It must be cleansed by sorrow's art,
Ere it will yield a fragrance sweet,
Ere it will shine a jewel meet
To lay before Thy dear Lord's feet!"

HYMN

O HOLY Saviour, Friend unseen,
The faint, the weak, on Thee may lean
Help me, throughout Life's varying scene,
By faith to cling to Thee!

Blest with communion so Divine,
Take what Thou wilt, shall I repine,
When as the branches to the vine,
My soul may cling to Thee?

Far from her home, fatigued, opprest,
Here she has found a place of rest,
An exile still, yet not unblest,
While she can cling to Thee!

Without a murmur I dismiss
My former dreams of earthly bliss;
My joy, my recompense be this,
Each hour to cling to Thee!

What though the world deceitful prove,
And earthly friends and joys remove,
With patient, uncomplaining love,
Still would I cling to Thee!

Oft when I seem to tread alone
Some barren waste with thorns o'ergrown,
A voice of love, in gentlest tone,
Whispers, "Still cling to Me!"

Though faith and hope awhile be tried,
I ask not, need not, aught beside;
How safe, how calm, how satisfied,
The souls that cling to Thee!

They fear not Life's rough storms to brave,
Since Thou art near, and strong to save;
Nor shudder e'en at Death's dark wave,
Because they cling to Thee!

Blest is my lot, whate'er befall;
What can disturb me, who appal;
While, as my strength, my rock, my all,
Saviour, I cling to Thee!

"COME UNTO ME!"

ART thou weary? Art thou languid?
  Art thou sore distrest?
"Come to Me," saith One, "and coming,
    Be at rest!"

Hath He marks to lead me to Him,
  If He be my Guide?
"In His feet and hands are wound-prints,
    And His side."

Is there diadem as monarch
  That His brow adorns?
"Yea, a crown in very surety,
    But of thorns!"

If I find Him, if I follow,
  What His guerdon here?
"Many a sorrow, many a labor,
    Many a tear."

If I still hold closely to Him,
  What hath He at last?
"Sorrow vanquished, labor ended,
    Jordan past!"

If I ask Him to receive me,
  Will He say me nay?
"Not till earth and not till Heaven
    Pass away!"

Tending, following, keeping, struggling,
Is He sure to bless?
"Angels, martyrs, prophets, pilgrims,
Answer—Yes!"

THE UNSEEN BATTLE-FIELD.

THERE is an unseen battle-field
In every human breast,
Where two opposing forces meet,
And where they seldom rest.

That field is hid from mortal sight,
'Tis only seen by One,
Who knows alone where victory lies
When each day's fight is done.

One army clusters strong and fierce,
Their chief of demon form;
His brow is like the thunder-cloud,
His voice the bursting storm.

His captains, Pride, and Lust, and Hate,
Whose troops watch night and day;
Swift to detect the weakest point,
And thirsting for the fray.

Contending with this mighty force
  Is but a little band;
Yet there, with an unquailing front,
  Those warriors firmly stand.

Their leader is of God-like form,
  Of countenance serene;
And glowing on His naked breast
  A single cross is seen.

His captains, Faith, and Hope, and Love
  Point to that wondrous sign,
And, gazing on it, all receive
  Strength from a source Divine.

They feel it speaks a glorious truth,
  A truth as great as sure,
That, to be victors, they must learn
  To love, confide, endure.

That faith sublime, in wildest strife,
  Imparts a holy calm;
For every deadly blow a shield,
  For every wound a balm.

And when they win that battle-field,
  Past toil is quite forgot;
The plain where carnage once had reigned,
  Become a hallowed spot.

The spot where joy of flowers and peace
  Spring from the fertile sod,
And breathe the perfume of their praise
  On every breeze of God!

WITHOUT MONEY AND WITHOUT PRICE

AN INVITATION.

COME to Jesus! Are you lonely?
  Solace sweet He will afford.
Lean on Jesus—Jesus only!
  Come, and find a loving Lord!

Are your trials past the telling?
  Are your sins as crimson dye?
Jesus sees your sad heart swelling,
  'Neath accusing Memory.

He is waiting—will you leave Him
  Pleading at your heart in vain?
He is willing—oh, believe Him!
  He may never call again.

He hath never yet forsaken
  One who trusts alone in God;
He your life-long debt hath taken,
  And hath paid it with His Blood.

From your sins He waits to cleanse you—
  You! the slave by Satan bound;
Messages of love He sends you—
  Where can such a Friend be found?

Are you sick? His word can heal you.
  Are you weary with the strife?
Are you hungry? He can fill you
  With the Heavenly Bread of Life!

Now! it is the time to try it:
  Test Him by His written Word;
Come, for He will ne'er deny it;
  Come to Christ, the Risen Lord!

Do you fear His sharp reproving
  That you did not go before;
That you left Him—so unloving—
  Waiting long time at your door?

He will only smile and greet you,
  Chasing shadows from your brow;
He will surely run to meet you,
  Saying, "Thou art welcome now!"

By still waters He will lead you,
  In green pastures you shall rest;
And the piercéd hands that freed you,
  Bear you on His tender breast.

Come, oh, come, this day, and try it!
  Jesus' words are proved and true;
Take His gift, you cannot buy it—
  He hath waited long for you.

"LOOKING UNTO JESUS."

THOU, Lord, my path shalt choose,
      And my Guide be!
What shall I fear to lose
      While I have Thee?
This be my portion blest,
On my Redeemer's breast,
In peaceful trust to rest:
      He cares for me!

Shall, I then, choose my way?
      Never, oh, no!
I, a creature of a day,
      What can I know?
What dread perplexity,
Then would encompass me;
Now I can look to Thee,
      Thou orderest so!

This lightens every cross,
      Cheers every ill;

Suffer I grief or loss,
It is Thy will!
Who can make no mistake,
Chooseth the way I take;
He who can ne'er forsake,
Holds my hand still!

Sweet words of peace and love
Christ whispers me!
Bearing my soul above
Life's troubled sea!
This be my portion blest,
On my Redeemer's breast
In peaceful trust to rest:
He cares for me!

Christ died my love to win,
Christ is my tower!
He will be with me in
Each trying hour!
He makes the wounded whole,
He will my heart console,
He will uphold my soul
By His own power!

To Thee, the only Wise,
Whatever be,
I will lift up mine eyes
Joyful in Thee!

This be my portion blest,
On my Redeemer's breast
In peaceful trust to rest:
He cares for me!

THE SPIRITUAL TEMPLE.

AND whither came these goodly stones
'Twas Israel's pride to raise
The glory of the former house,
The joy of ancient days;
In purity and strength erect,
In radiant splendor bright,
Sparkling with golden beams of noon,
Or silver smiles of night?

From coasts the stately cedar crowns
Each noble slab was brought,
In Lebanon's deep quarries hewn,
And on its mountains wrought;
There rung the hammer's heavy stroke
Among the echoing rocks;
There chased the chisel's keen, sharp edge,
The rude, unshapen blocks.

Thence polished, perfected, complete,
Each fitted to its place,

For lofty coping, massive walls,
  Or deep imbedded base—
They bore them o'er the waves that rolled
  Their billowy swell between
The shores of Tyre's imperial pride,
  And Judah's hills of green.

With gradual toil the work went on,
  Through days, and months, and years,
Beneath the Summer's laughing sun,
  And Winter's frozen tears.
And thus in majesty sublime
  And noiseless pomp it rose—
Fit dwelling for the God of peace!
  A temple of repose.

Brethren in Christ, to holier things
  The simple type apply;
Our God himself a temple builds,
  Eternal, and on high,
Of ransomed souls · their Zion there—
  That world of light and bliss—
Their Lebanon, the place of toil,
  Of previous moulding—this!

From Nature's quarries, deep and dark,
  With gracious aim He hews
The stones, the spiritual stones,
  It pleaseth Him to choose.

Hard, rugged, shapeless at the first,
Yet destined each to shine—
Moulded beneath His patient hand—
In purity divine.

Oh, glorious process! see the proud
Grow lowly, gentle, meek;
See floods of unaccustomed tears
Gush down the hardened cheek:
Perchance the hammer's heavy stroke
O'erthrew some idol fond;
Perchance the chisel rent in twain
Some precious, tender bond.

Behold, he prays! Whose lips were sealed
In quiet scorn before,
Sighs for the closet's holy calm,
And hails the welcome door.
Behold, he works for Jesus now,
Whose days went idly past;
Oh, for more mouldings of the Hand
That works a change so vast!

Ye looked on one, a well-wrought stone,
A saint of God matured.
What chiselings that heart had felt!
What chastening strokes endured!

But marked ye not that last soft touch
  What perfect grace it gave,
Ere Jesus bore His servant home
  Across the darksome wave?

Home to the place His grace designed
  That chosen soul to fill,
In the bright temple of the saved,
  Upon His holy hill.
Home to the noiselessness, the peace
  Of those sweet shrines above,
Whose stones shall never be displaced –
  Set in redeeming love.

Lord, chisel, chasten, polish us,
  Each blemish wash away;
Cleanse us with purifying blood,
  In spotless robes array;
And thus, Thine image on us stamped,
  Transport us to the shore
Where not a stroke is ever felt,
  For none is needed more.

ONLY OUR LOVE

TO do Thy holy will;
  To bear Thy cross;
To trust Thy mercy still,
  In pain or loss;

Poor gifts are these to bring,
  Dear Lord, to Thee,
Who hast done everything
      For me!

For Thy belovéd Son
  And precious Word;
For all Thy goodness done
  On earth, O Lord!
For leave that I may live,—
  Blest boon of Thine,—
What recompense can give
  This heart of mine?

What, for Thy glorious earth,—
  Thy stars and flowers?
What, for Thy seasons' birth,
  Kind Lord of ours?
What, for the gentle ones
  Whose lives I share?
For home, and the kindly tones
  Love whispers there?

Thou, Who enthroned above
  Dost hear our call,
Oh, can our faithful love
  Pay Thee for all?

Poor recompense to bring,
  Dear Lord, to Thee,
Who hast done everything
  For me!

IN THE CLOSET.

THE air is stirred with holy life,
  All earthly thoughts take wing;
Hushed be the tumult of my heart.
  I hear the angels sing.

Yes! o'er my bowed and weeping head,
  I feel their waving wings,
While mercy-drops are falling round,
  Drops from the heavenly springs.

And softly from the holy haze
  Falls forth the word of cheer:
"Speak, troubled soul, what is thy need?
  Jesus Himself is here!"

"My Lord and God!" my soul replies,
  "I hear Thy gracious call;
No need have I, since Thou art here,
  Thou art my all in all!

"Oh, let me ever here repose
Upon Thy soothing breast;
For now I know how blissfully
Thy weary ones find rest!"

IN SUFFERING

FATHER, Thy will, not mine, be done;
So prayed on earth Thy suffering Son
So in His name I pray.
The spirit faints, the flesh is weak,
Thy help in agony I seek—
Oh, take this cup away!

If such be not Thy sov'reign will,
Thy wiser purpose then fulfill;
My wishes I resign,
Into Thy hands my soul commend,
On Thee for life or death depend;
Thy will be done, not mine.

AND THEY SHALL SEE HIS FACE.

WHAT must it be to dwell above,
At God's right hand, where Jesus reigns,
Since the sweet earnest of His love
O'erwhelms us on these dreary plains!

No heart can think, no tongue explain,
What bliss it is with Christ to reign.

When sin no more obstructs our sight,
When sorrow pains our heart no more,
How shall we view the Prince of Light,
And all His works of grace explore!
What heights and depths of love Divine
Will there through endless ages shine!

Well, He has fixed the happy day
When the last tears will wet our eyes,
And God shall wipe all tears away,
And fill us with Divine surprise
To hear His voice, and see His face,
And feel His infinite embrace!

This is the Heaven I long to know,
For this, with patience, I would wait,
Till, weaned from earth and all below,
I mount to my celestial seat,
And wave my palm, and wear my crown,
And, with the elders, cast them down.

IN THE OTHER WORLD.

IT lies around us like a cloud—
A world we do not see;
Yet the sweet closing of an eye
May bring us there to be.

Its gentle breezes fan our cheek;
  Amid our worldly cares
Its gentle voices whisper love,
  And mingle with our prayers.

Sweet hearts around us throb and beat,
  Sweet helping hands are stirred,
And palpitates the veil between
  With breathings almost heard.

The silence—awful, sweet, and calm—
  They have no power to break;
For mortal words are not for them
  To utter or partake.

So thin, so soft, so sweet they glide,
  So near to press they seem—
They seem to lull us to our rest,
  And melt into our dream.

And in the hush of rest they bring
  'Tis easy now to see
How lovely, and how sweet a pass,
  The hour of death may be.

To close the eye, and close the ear,
  Wrapped in a trance of bliss,
And gently dream in loving arms
  To swoon to that—from this.

Scarce knowing if we wake or sleep,
Scarce asking where we are,
To feel all evil sink away,
All sorrow and all care.

Sweet souls around us ! watch us still,
Press nearer to our side,
Into our thoughts, into our prayers,
With gentle helpings glide.

Let death between us be as naught,
A dried and vanished stream :
Your joy be the reality,
Our suffering life the dream.

CHRIST RISEN.

THE foe behind, the deep before,
Our hosts have dared and past the sea ;
And Pharoah's warriors strew the shore,
And Israel's ransomed tribes are free.
Lift up, lift up your voices now !
The whole wide-world rejoices now !
The Lord hath triumphed gloriously !
The Lord shall reign victoriously !
Happy morrow,
Turning sorrow
Into peace and mirth !

Bondage ending,
Love descending
O'er the earth!
Seals assuring,
Guard's securing
Watch his earthly prison,
Seals are shattered,
Guards are scattered,
Christ hath risen!

No longer must the mourners weep,
Nor call departed Christians dead;
For death is hallowed into sleep
And every grave becomes a bed.
Now once more
Eden's door
Open stands to mortal eyes;
For Christ hath risen, and men shall rise:
Now at last,
Old things past,
Hope, and joy, and peace begin:
For Christ hath won, and men shall win.

It is not exile, rest on high:
It is not sadness, peace from strife:
To fall asleep is not to die:
To dwell with Christ is better life.

Where our banner leads us,
 We may safely go·
Where our Chief precedes us,
 We may face the foe.
His right arm is o'er us,
 He will guide us through;
Christ hath gone before us;
 Christians! follow you!

---

*GLORY DWELLETH IN IMMANUEL'S LAND.**

I.

THE sands of time are sinking,
 The dawn of Heaven breaks,
The Summer morn I've sighed for,
 The fair sweet morn, awakes!

* Samuel Rutherford, a man of great learning and talents, was first a Professor in the University of Edinburgh, then minister of the parish of Anworth, and subsequently Professor of Theology at St. Andrew's, in Scotland. At one time he was imprisoned for the name of Jesus. His death-bed was as remarkable as his life had been. Some of his dying expressions are preserved by Mr. Fleming in his *Fulfilling of Scripture*, who thus concludes his narrative: "And thus, full of the Spirit, yea, as it were, overcome with sensible enjoyment, he breathed out his soul, his last words being: 'Glory, glory dwelleth in Immanuel's land!'"

Dark, dark hath been the midnight,
  But dayspring is at hand,
And glory—glory dwelleth
  In Immanuel's land.

II.

Oh, well it is for ever!
  Oh, well for evermore!
My nest hung in no forest
  Of all this death-doomed shore.
Yea, let the vain world vanish,
  As from the ship the strand,
While glory—glory dwelleth
  In Immanuel's land.

III.

There the Red Rose of Sharon
  Unfolds its heartsome bloom
And fills the air of Heaven
  With ravishing perfume:
Oh, to behold it blossom,
  While by its fragrance fanned
While glory—glory dwelleth
  In Immanuel's land.

IV.

The King there, in His beauty,
  Without a vail, is seen:

It were a well-spent journey,
  Though seven deaths lay between.
The Lamb, with His fair army,
  Doth on Mount Zion stand,
And glory—glory dwelleth
  In Immanuel's land

V.

Oh, Christ He is the Fountain,
  The deep sweet well of love!
The streams on earth I've tasted,
  More deep I'll drink above:
There, to an ocean fulness,
  His mercy doth expand,
And glory—glory dwelleth
  In Immanuel's land.

VI.

E'en Anworth was not heaven—
  E'en preaching was not Christ;
And in my sea-beat prison
  My Lord and I held tryst:
And aye my murkiest storm-cloud
  Was by a rainbow spanned,
Caught from the glory dwelling
  In Immanuel's land.

VII.

But that He built a heaven
  Of His surpassing love,
A little New Jerusalem,
  Like to the one above—
"Lord, take me o'er the water,"
  Had been my loud demand;
"Take me to love's own country,
  Unto Immanuel's land."

VIII.

But flowers need night's cool darkness,
  The moonlight and the dew;
So Christ, from one who loved it,
  His shining oft withdrew:
And then, for cause of absence,
  My troubled soul I scanned—
But glory, shadeless, shineth
  In Immanuel's land.

IX.

The little birds at Anworth
  I used to count them blest—
Now, beside happier altars
  I go to build my nest:
O'er these there broods no silence,
  No graves around them stand,
For glory, deathless, dwelleth
  In Immanuel's land.

X.

Fair Anworth by the Solway,
  To me thou still art dear!
E'en from the verge of Heaven
  I drop for thee a tear.
Oh, if one soul from Anworth
  Meet me at God's right hand,
My heaven will be two heavens
  In Immanuel's land.

XI.

I've wrestled on toward Heaven,
  'Gainst storm, and wind, and tide
Now, like a weary traveler,
  That leaneth on his guide,
Amid the shades of evening,
  While sinks life's lingering sand,
I hail the glory dawning
  From Immanuel's land.

XII.

Deep waters crossed life's pathway,
  The hedge of thorns was sharp:
Now, these lie all behind me—
  Oh, for a well-tuned harp!
Oh, to join Hallelujah
  With yon triumphant band,
Who sing, where glory dwelleth,
  In Immanuel's land

XIII.

With mercy and with judgment
  My web of time He wove,
And aye the dews of sorrow
  Were lustered with His love:
I'll bless the Hand that guided,
  I'll bless the Heart that planned,
When throned where glory dwelleth,
  In Immanuel's land.

XIV.

Soon shall the cup of glory
  Wash down earth's bitterest woes,
Soon shall the desert's brier
  Break into Eden's rose;
The curse shall change to blessing—
  The name on earth that's banned,
Be graven on the white stone
  In Immanuel's land.

XV.

Oh, I am my Belovéd's,
  And my Beloved is mine!
He brings a poor vile sinner
  Into His "house of wine!"
I stand upon His merit,
  I know no safer stand,
Not e'en where glory dwelleth
  In Immanuel's land.

XVI.

I shall sleep sound in Jesus,
  Filled with His likeness rise,
To live and to adore Him,
  To see Him with these eyes:
'Tween me and resurrection
  But Paradise doth stand;
Then—then for glory dwelling.
  In Immanuel's land.

XVII.

The bride eyes not her garments,
  But her dear bridegroom's face;
I will not gaze at glory,
  But on my King of Grace—
Not at the crown He giveth,
  But on His piercèd hand:
The Lamb is all the glory
  Of Immanuel's land.

XVIII.

I have borne scorn and hatred,
  I have borne wrong and shame
Earth's proud ones have reproached me,
  For Christ's thrice-blessèd name:
Where God's seal set the fairest,
  They've stamped their foulest brand;
But judgment shines like noonday
  In Immanuel's land.

SURELY I COME QUICKLY

O'ER the distant mountains breaking,
Comes the reddening dawn of day;
Rise, my soul, from sleep awaking,
Rise and sing, and watch, and pray,—
'Tis thy Saviour,
On His bright returning way.

O Thou long-expected, weary
Waits my anxious soul for Thee!
Life is dark, and earth is dreary,
Where Thy light I do not see.
O my Saviour,
When wilt Thou return to me!

Long, too long, in sin and sadness,
Far away from Thee I pine;
When, oh, when shall I the gladness
Of Thy Spirit feel in mine!
O my Saviour,
When shall I be wholly Thine!

Heaven is my soul's salvation;
Spent the night the day at hand;
Keep me in my lowly station,
Watching for Thee, till I stand,
O my Saviour,
In Thy bright and promised land!

With my lamp well trimmed and burning,
Swift to hear, and slow to roam,
Watching for Thy glad returning,
To restore me to my home,
Come, my Saviour—
O my Saviour, quickly come!

"HE GOETH BEFORE THEM."

THE winds blow fierce across the barren wild;
The storm-clouds gather darkly on our way;
'Tis cold! But, oh, that loving face and mild,
Which goes before! *there* first the shadows stay
And tempests reach Him first, our Shepherd there
What He endures shall we complain to bear?

The night comes on—'tis dark! the stars are dim,
We cannot see the way! But, oh, that form
Which goes before! the night comes *first* to Him·
And darkness first is His,—as was the storm!
Shall we shrink back, or tremble to go on,
Where He, our Shepherd, first for us hath gone?

The way is rough, and wearying steeps arise;
And thorns are there to wound our aching feet.
But, oh, those sacred footsteps, firm and wise,
Which go before! they first the roughness meet,

And briers reach them first! Oh, shall we dread
To bear *His* cross—to walk where *He* hath led?

The stream is reached;—the river dark and cold;
  The waves are high! But, oh, that mighty One,
Who goes before!—the billows o'er *Him* rolled;
  He crossed the waters first, and shall we shun
The final anguish which our Shepherd bore?
His hand shall guide us to the other shore!

He goes *before!* And so we may not look
  Backward at all, but onward evermore;
Keeping in sight the blessèd path He took,
  Patient to bear each cross He meekly bore;
Trusting His wisdom in the darkest hour;
O'ercoming every trial through His power!

He goes before! a shield against the storm:
  A shadow in the noon-day,—lights at night;
In danger's hour, there is the Shepherd's form
  But just beyond; though fears may dim our
      sight,
Oh, earthly flock, fear not forevermore!
Where'er we walk, our Shepherd "goes before."

HIS NAME

O WONDERFUL! round whose birth-hour
Prophetic song, miraculous power,
Cluster and hum, like star and flower.

Those marvelous rays that at Thy will,
From the closed Heaven which is so chill,
So passionless, stream'd round Thee still,

Are but as broken gleams that start,
O Light of lights, from Thy deep heart,
Thyself, Thyself, the Wonder art!

O Counselor! four thousand years,
One question, tremulous with tears,
One awful question, vexed our peers.

They ask'd the vault, but no one spoke;
They ask'd the depth, no answer woke;
They ask'd their hearts, that only broke.

They look'd, and sometimes on the height
Far off they saw a haze of white,
That was a storm, but look'd like light.

The secret of the years is read,
The' enigma of the quick and dead
By the child-voice interpreted.

O everlasting Father, God!
Sun after sun went down, and trod
Race after race the green earth's sod,

'Till generations seemed to be
But dead waves of an endless sea,
But dead leaves from a deathless tree.

But Thou hast come, and now we know
Each wave hath an eternal flow,
Each leaf a lifetime after snow.

O Prince of Peace! crown'd, yet discrown'd,
They say no war nor battle's sound
Was heard the tired world around;

They say the hour that Thou didst come
The trumpet's voice was stricken dumb,
And no one beat the battle-drum.

Yea, still as life to them that mark.
Its poor adventure seems a bark,
Whose track is pale, whose sail is dark,

Thou who art Wonderful dost fling
One ray, till like a sea-bird's wing
The canvas is a snowy thing,—

Till the dark boat is turn'd to gold,
The sunlit-silver'd ocean rolled
With anthems that are new and old,

With noble path of luminous ray
From the boat slanting all the way,
To the island of undying day.

And still as clouding questions swarm
Around our hearts, and dimly form
Their problems of the mist and storm;

And still as ages fleet, but fraught
With syllables, whereby is wrought
The fullness of the Eternal thought;

And when not yet in God's sunshine,
The smoke drifts from the embattled line
Of warning hearts that would be Thine!

We bid our doubts and passions cease,
Our restless fears be still'd with these—
Counsellor, Father, Prince of Peace!

THE E'EN BRINGS A' HAME.

UPON the hills the wind is sharp and cold,
The sweet young grasses wither on the wold,
And we, O Lord! have wander'd from Thy fold;
But evening brings us home.

Among the mists we stumbled, and the rocks
Where the brown lichen whitens, and the fox
Watches the straggler from the scattered flocks;
But evening brings us home.

The sharp thorns prick us, and our tender feet
Are cut and bleeding, and the lambs repeat
Their pitiful complaints—oh, rest is sweet
When evening brings us home.

We have been wounded by the hunters' darts;
Our eyes are very heavy, and our hearts
Search for Thy coming—when the light departs
At evening, bring us home.

The darkness gathers. Through the gloom no star
Rises to guide us. We have wander'd far—
Without Thy lamp we know not where we are;
At evening bring us home.

The clouds are round us, and the snow-drifts
thicken:
O Thou, dear Shepherd! leave us not to sicken
In the waste night; our tardy footsteps quicken,
At evening bring us home.

KNOCKING, EVER KNOCKING.

[Suggested by Hunt's Picture of the "LIGHT OF THE WORLD.]

"Behold, I stand at the door and knock!"

KNOCKING, knocking, ever knocking!
Who is there?
'Tis a pilgrim, strange and kingly,
Never such was seen before;—
Ah, sweet soul, for such a wonder
Undo the door.

No! that door is hard to open;
Hinges rusty, latch is broken;
Bid Him go.
Wherefore, with that knocking dreary
Scare the sleep from one so weary?
Say Him—no.

Knocking, knocking, ever knocking?
What! Still there?
Oh, sweet soul, but once behold Him,
With the glory-crownéd hair;

And those eyes, so strange and tender,
　　Waiting there;
Open! Open! Once behold Him—
　　Him, so fair!

Ah, that door! Why wilt Thou vex me,
Coming ever to perplex me?
For the key is stiffly rusty,
And the bolt is clogg'd and dusty;
Many-finger'd ivy vine
Seals it fast with twist and twine;
Weeds of years, and years before,
Choke the passage of that door.

Knocking, knocking! What? Still knocking?
　　He still there?
What's the hour? The night is waning—
In my heart a drear complaining,
　　And a chilly, sad unrest!
Ah, this knocking! It disturbs me!
Scares my sleep with dreams unblest!
　　Give me rest:
　　Rest—ah, rest!

Rest, dear soul, He longs to give thee;
Thou hast only dream'd of pleasure—
Dream'd of gifts and golden treasure—
Dream'd of jewels in thy keeping,

Waked to weariness of weeping;—
Open to thy soul's one Lover,
And thy night of dreams is over,—
The true gifts He brings have seeming
More than all thy faded dreaming!

Did she open? Doth she? Will she?
So, as wondering we behold,
Grows the picture to a sign,
Press'd upon your soul and mine;
For in every breast that liveth
Is that strange mysterious door;—
The forsaken and betangled,
Ivy-gnarled and weed-bejangled,
Dusty, rusty, and forgotten;—
There the piercèd hand still knocketh,
And with ever patient watching,
With the sad eyes true and tender,
With the glory-crownèd hair,—
Still a God is waiting there.

JACOB'S LADDER.

AH! many a time we look on starlit-nights
Up to the sky, as Jacob did of old;
Look longing up to the eternal lights,
To spell their lives of gold.

But never more, as to the Hebrew boy,
  Each on his way the Angels walk abroad,
And never more we hear, with awful joy,
    Tho' audible voice of God.

Yet, to pure eyes the ladder still is set,
  And Angel visitants still come and go;
Many bright messengers are moving yet
    From the dark world below.

Thoughts, that are surely Faith's outspreading wings—
  Prayers of the Church, aye keeping time and tryst—
Heart-wishes, making bee-like murmurings,
    Their flower the Eucharist.

Spirits elect, through suffering render'd meet
  For those high mansions—from the nursery-door
Bright babes that seem to climb with clay-cold feet,
    Up to the Golden Floor—

These are the messengers, forever wending
  From earth to Heaven, that faith alone may scan;
These are the Angels of our God, ascending
    Upon the Son of Man!

MARAH.

GOD sends us bitter, that the sweet,
  By absence known, may sweeter prove;
As dark for light, as cold for heat,
        Brings greater love.

God sends us bitter, as to show
  He can both sweet and bitter send;
That both the might and love we know
        Of our great Friend.

He sends us bitter, lest too gay
  We wreathe around our heads the rose,
And count our right, what Heaven each day
        As alms bestows.

God sends us bitter, lest we fail
  That bitterest Grief aright to prize
Which did for all the world avail
        In His own eyes.

God sends us bitter, all our sins
Embittering; yet so kindly sends,
The path that bitterness begins
        In sweetness ends.

He sends us bitter, that Heaven's sweet,
  Earth's bitter o'er, may sweeter taste:
As Canaan's ground to Israel's feet,
    For that great waste.

Our passions murmur and rebel,
  But Faith cries out unto the Lord,
And prayer by patience worketh well
    Its own reward.

For, if our heart the lesson draws
  Aright, by bitter chastening taught,
To keep His statutes and His laws
    Even as we ought,

He openeth our eyes to see
  (Eyes that our pride of heart had seal'd)
The sweetness of Life's heavenly Tree,
    And grief is heal'd.

And lo! before us in the way
  We view the fountains and the palms,
And drink, and pitch our tents, and stay
    Singing sweet psalms.

PER PACEM AD LUCEM.

I DO not ask, O Lord! that life may be
A pleasant road;
I do not ask that Thou wouldst take from me
Aught of its load;
I do not ask that flowers should always spring
Beneath my feet;
I know too well the poison and the sting
Of things too sweet.
For one thing only, Lord, dear Lord! I plead:
Lead me aright—
Though strength should falter, and though heart
should bleed—
Through Peace to Light.

I do not ask, O Lord! that Thou shouldst shed
Full radiance here;
Give but a ray of Peace, that I may tread
Without a fear.
I do not ask my cross to understand,
My way to see,—
Better in darkness just to feel Thy Hand,
And follow Thee.
Joy is like restless day, but Peace Divine
Like quiet night.
Lead me, O Lord! till perfect Day shall shine,
Through Peace to Light.

"EVEN AS THOU WILT."

"HAVE mercy on me, Lord!"
She followed Him, and cried; and when
there came
No answer, follow'd, crying still the same,—
"Have mercy on me, Lord!"

"Send her away," they said—
They who should be dispensers of His grace,
Would have Him turn from her who sought His
face:
"Send her away," they said.

He spoke their thought aloud—
"It is not meet to take the children's bread
And cast it to the dogs"—as if He said,
"How poor ye are and proud."

"Yea, Lord! and yet the dogs
Eat of the crumbs that from the children fall,"
She pleaded—"and there is enough for all—
For children and for dogs."

And He to her replied,
"Even as Thou wilt, so be it unto Thee.
Thy heart the measure of the grace shall be
From my rich store supplied."

She had the thing she would—
Lord! if I dip my cup into the sea,
It rises full. Such cup each soul may be,
Such Ocean is Thy good!

THE TWO SUNSETS.

NO bird-song floated down the hill,
The tangled bank below was still;

No rustle from the birchen stem,
No ripple from the water's hem.

The dusk of twilight round us grew
We felt the falling of the dew;

For, from us, ere the day was done,
The wooded hills shut out the sun.

But on the river's farther side,
We saw the hill-tops glorified:

A tender glow, exceeding fair,
A dream of day without its glare.

With us the damp, the chill, the gloom;
With them the sunset's rosy bloom;

While dark, through willowy vistas seen,
The river rolled in shade between.

From out the darkness, where we trod,
We gazed upon those hills of God,

Whose light seemed not of moon or sun;
We spake not, but our thought was one.

We paused, as if from that bright shore
Beckoned our dear ones gone before;

And stilled our beating hearts to hear
The voices lost to mortal ear!

Sudden our pathway turned from night;
The hills swung open to the light;

Thro' their green gates the sunshine showed
A long, slant splendor downward flowed.

Down glade, and glen, and bank it rolled:
It bridged the shaded stream with gold,

And, borne on piers of mist, allied
The shadowy with the sunlit side!

"So," prayed we, "when our feet draw near
The river, dark with mortal fear,

And the night cometh, chill with dew,
O Father! let Thy light break through!

So let the hills of doubt divide,
So bridge with faith the sunless tide!

So let the eyes that fail on earth
On Thy eternal hills look forth;

And, in Thy beckoning angels, know
The dear ones whom we loved below!"

WHY DOST THOU WAIT?

POOR trembling lamb! Ah, who outside the fold
Has bid thee stand, all weary as thou art?
Dangers around thee, and the bitter cold
Creeping and growing to thine inmost heart;
Who bids thee wait till some mysterious feeling,
Thou know'st not what—perchance may never know—
Shall find thee where in darkness thou art kneeling,
And fill thee with a rich and wondrous glow
Of love and faith; and change to warmth and light
The chill and darkness of thy spirit's night?

For miracles like this, who bids thee wait?
  Behold, "The Spirit and the Bride say, Come!"
The tender Shepherd opens wide the gate,
  And in His love would gently lead thee home.
Why shouldst thou wait? Long centuries ago,
  Thou timid lamb, the Shepherd paid for thee.
Thou art His own. Wouldst thou His beauty
    know,
  Nor trust the love which yet thou canst not see?
Thou hast not learned this lesson to receive;
  More bless'd are they who see not, yet believe.

Still dost thou wait for feeling? Dost thou say,
  "Fain would I love and trust, but hope is dead;
I have no faith, and without faith, who may
  Rest in the blessing which is only shed
Upon the faithful? I must stand and wait."
  Not so. The Shepherd does not ask of thee
Faith in thy faith, but only faith in Him.
  And this He meant in saying, "Come to Me!"
In light or darkness seek to do His will,
  And leave the work of faith to Jesus still.

THE EVERLASTING MEMORIAL

UP and away, like the dew of the morning,
  That soars from the earth to its home in the sun,—
So let me steal away, gently and lovingly,
  Only remembered by what I have done.

My name, and my place, and my tomb all forgotten,
  The brief race of time well and patiently run,
So let me pass away, peacefully, silently,
  Only remembered by what I have done.

Gladly away from this toil would I hasten,
  Up to the crown that for me has been won;
Unthought of by man in rewards or in praises,—
  Only remembered by what I have done.

Up and away, like the odors of sunset,
  That sweeten the twilight as darkness comes on;
So be my life,—a thing felt but not noticed,
  And I but remembered by what I have done.

Yes, like the fragrance that wanders in freshness,
  When the flowers that it came from are closed up and gone;

So would I be to this world's weary dwellers,
  Only remembered by what I have done.

Needs there the praise of the love-written record,
  The name and the epitaph graved on the stone?
The things we have lived for,—let them be our story,
  We ourselves but remembered by what we have done.

I need not be missed, if my life has been bearing
  (As its Summer and Autumn moved silently on)
The bloom, and the fruit, and the seed of its season;
  I shall still be remembered by what I have done.

I need not be missed, if another succeed me,
  To reap down those fields which in Spring I have sown;
He who plowed and who sowed is not missed by the reaper,
  He is only remembered by what he has done.

Not myself, but the truth that in life I have spoken,
  Not myself, but the seed that in life I have sown,
Shall pass on to ages,—all about me forgotten,
  Save the truth I have spoken, the things I have done.

So let my living be, so be my dying;
So let my name lie, unblazoned, unknown;
Unpraised and unmissed, I shall still be remembered;
Yes,—but remembered by what I have done.

THE TWO VILLAGES

OVER the river on the hill
Lieth a village white and still;
All around it the forest-trees
Shiver and whisper in the breeze;
Over it sailing shadows go
Of soaring hawk and screaming crow,
And mountain grasses, low and sweet,
Grow in the middle of every street.

Over the river under the hill
Another village lieth still;
There I see in the cloudy night
Twinkling stars of household light,
Fires that gleam from the smithy's door,
Mists that curl on the river's shore;
And in the roads no grasses grow,
For the wheels that hasten to and fro.

In that village on the hill
Never is sound of smithy or mill

The houses are thatched with grass and flowers,
Never a clock to tell the hours;
The marble doors are always shut;
You may not enter at hall or hut;
All the village lie asleep;
Never a grain to sow or reap;
Never in dreams to moan or sigh,
Silent, and idle, and low they lie.

In that village under the hill,
When the night is starry and still,
Many a weary soul in prayer
Looks to the other village there,
And weeping and sighing, longs to go
Up to *that* home, from this below;
Longs to sleep by the forest wild,
Whither have vanished wife and child,
And heareth, praying, this answer fall—
"Patience! that village shall hold ye all!"

THE WAYSIDE WATCHER.

"ALL the day you sit here idle,
And the Master at the door!
The fields are white to harvest,
And our labor almost o'er.
You are dreaming, you are dreaming!
Time is gliding fast away;

See! the eventide is waning,
  Soon shall break eternal day."

"Brother, my hand is feeble,
  My strength is well-nigh spent:
I saw you all at noon-day,
  And I marked the way ye went
I cried, 'God's blessing on them,
  What a favored band they be!
But I'll watch upon the highway,
  God may find a work for me.'"

"Yet you tarry, yet you tarry,"
  Said the laborer again,
"You may idle on the highway,
  And wait all day in vain.
'Tis easy labor 'waiting;'
  On the dusty road we tread
To toil within the vineyard:
  Go out and work instead."

The watcher smiled and answered,
  "My brother, is it so?
Who waiteth on the Master,
  The Master's will shall know.
He hath taught me one sweet lesson,
  I have learnt it not too late,
There is service for the feeblest
  That only stand and wait."

I sat me by the hedge-row,
  No burden could I bear,
But I often thought, how blessèd
  In the field to have a share!
The loving Master whispered,
  Through the often lonely day,
"Still wait on Me, thou weak one,
  The lame shall take the prey."

Not long I tarried watching:
  A wayfarer drew nigh,
He was weary, sad, and hungry,
  For the glowing sun was high.
His foot lagged faint and fainter,
  His eyes were downward cast;
That laborer by my lattice
  At early morn had passed.

I drew him 'neath the trellis
  Of the vine's inviting shade,
Down by the soft green pasture
  Our Shepherd's love hath made.
I fetched him from the streamlet
  Fresh water for his feet,
I spread the bread before him,
  And bade him rest and eat.

He bathed in the bright fountain,
  And then refreshed and strong,

He journeyed on rejoicing:
  You could hear his happy song.
Where, on the dusty wayside,
  The traveler had been,
Stood One, in heavenly beauty,
  With more than regal mien.

"I thank thee," said the Stranger,
  "For all thy cares afford,
For rest, and food, and welcome,
  Beside thy simple board."
"Nay, Lord," I said, "what succor
  Have I bestowed on Thee?"
"Thy service to my servant
  Hath all been done to Me."

Oh, it was well worth watching,
  A Summer's day alone;
Well worth the weary waiting,
  To hear His sweet "Well done!"
Is it too small a matter,
  That in man's foolish pride
He scorns one heart to gladden
  For which the Saviour died?

Oh, ever blessèd Master!
  The harvest-field is fair,
And Thou hast better servants,
  Than Thy weak one, everywhere.

Thou never hast forsaken
  One waiting by the way ;
Still meet me with a promise,
  That the lame shall take the prey.

From the tangled thicket near me
  I heard a mournful cry ;
A little child had wandered
  From the sunny path hard by :
His hands were torn with briers,
  His hot tears fell like rain ;
And he wept, lest he should never
  See his father's face again.

Close to my heart I drew him,
  And pointed to the sky ;
I showed him how the dark clouds,
  So slowly sailing by,
But veiled the bright sun's radiance
  From valley and from hill ;
For the faithful sun was shining
  In all his glory still !

He ceased to weep, and listened ;
  I soothed his childish woe ;
Then on the way I led him,
  And soon beheld him go

Back through the green fields singing:
  Sweet was the joyful sound,
That told the father's welcome,
  And the little wanderer found!

Then on the highway, near me,
  I saw the Stranger stand—
Stranger no more! He guided
  The fair child by the hand.
"I thank thee," said He softly,
  "Thou hast not watched in vain;
Behold my child returnéd
  Safe to my arms again."

What grace is Thine, O Master!
  For work so poor and scant;
How glorious is the guerdon
  My loving Lord doth grant!
I only saw a nursling
  Was wandering astray:
Oh, it is worth cross-bearing
  To wait for Thee one day!

Have ye known the shadows darken
  On weary nights of pain,
And hours that seem to lengthen
  Till the night comes round again?

The folded hands seem idle:
  If folded at His word,
'Tis a holy service, trust me,
  In obedience to the Lord.

Ye know the joy of labor
  Within the busy field;
But there are deeper pleasures
  A faithful heart may yield.
To willing ones that suffer,
  And listen at His feet,
From the far-off land God giveth
  The fruit of life to eat.

Brief is my hour of labor:
  My Lord my lot hath cast:
He giveth royal wages
  To the first-called as the last.
I have seen Him in His beauty,
  While waiting here alone—
I know Him ever near me,
  For He cannot leave His own.

None e'er shall lack a service,
  Who only seek His will;
And He doth teach His children
  To suffer and be still.

In love's deep fount of treasures
  Such precious things are stored,
Laid up for you, O blessèd
  That wait upon the Lord!

CAST DOWN BUT NOT DESTROYED.

MUCH have I borne, but not as I should bear;
The proud will unsubdued, the formal prayer
Tell me Thou yet wilt chide, Thou canst not spare
    O Lord, Thy chastening rod!
O help me, Father! for my sinful heart
Back from this discipline of grief would start,
Unmindful of His sorer, deeper smart,
    Who died for me, my God!

Yet if each wish denied, each woe and pain,
Break but some link of that oppressive chain
Which binds us still to earth, and leaves a stain
    Thou only canst remove—
Then am I blest—oh, bliss from man concealed!
If here to Christ, the weak one's tower and shield,
My heart through sorrow be set free to yield
    A service of deep love.

ABOUNDING IN HOPE.

HOPE, Christian soul! in every stage
Of this, thine earthly pilgrimage,
Let heavenly joy thy thoughts engage—
Abound in hope.

Hope! though thy lot be want and woe,
Though hate's rude storms against thee blow,
Thy Saviour's lot was such below—
Abound in hope.

Hope! for to all who meekly bear
His cross, He gives His crown to wear;
Abasement here is glory there—
Abound in hope.

Hope! though thy dear ones round thee die,
Behold with Faith's illumined eye
Their deathless home beyond the sky—
Abound in hope.

Hope! for upon that happy shore
Sorrow and sighing will be o'er,
And friends shall meet to part no more—
Abound in hope.

Hope through the watches of the night:
Hope till the morrow bring the light:
Hope till thy faith be lost in sight—
Abound in hope.

"HE GIVETH SONGS IN THE NIGHT."

WE praise Thee oft for hours of bliss,
For days of quiet rest:
But, oh, how seldom do we feel
That pain and tears are best!

We praise Thee for the shining sun,
For kind and gladsome ways:
When shall we learn, O Lord! to sing
Through weary nights and days.

We praise Thee when our path is plain
And smooth beneath our feet;
But fain would learn to welcome pain,
And call the bitter sweet.

When rises first the blush of hope,
Our hearts begin to sing;
But surely not for this alone
Should we our gladness bring.

Are there no hours of conflict fierce.
  No weary toils and pains,
No watchings, and no bitterness,
  That bring their blessèd gains?

That bring their blessèd gains full well,
  In truer faith and love,
And patience sweet, and gentleness,
  From our dear Home above!

Teach Thou our weak and wandering hearts
  Aright to read Thy way,—
That Thou with loving hand dost trace
  Our history every day.

Then every thorny crown of care
  Worn well in patience now,
Shall grow a glorious diadem
  Upon the faithful brow;

And every word of grief shall change
  And wave a blessèd flower,
And lift its face beneath our feet
  To bless us every hour;

And Sorrow's face shall be unveiled,
  And we at last shall see
Her eyes are eyes of tenderness,
  Her speech but echoes Thee!

NEAREST AND DEAREST.

'T was the Sabbath's blessèd evening hour,
And the dusk stillness of the fire-lit room
Fell on the spirit with a soothing power,
A spell of holy calm unmixed with gloom.
The fire-light flickered upon steadfast eyes,
Brows where the Prince of Peace his seal had set.
And tremulous lips where echoes of the skies,
Most eloquent in silence, lingered yet.

At length the musing of one heart found way;
"Oh, it is bliss!" she said, "to join the throng
That fills God's temple on His holy day,
With the full harmony of sacred song.
Surely the soul draws nearest to Him there,
And bows with holiest awe before His throne;
Surely the highest bliss of faith and prayer
Is found within those sacred courts alone!"

"Nay," said another, "not *alone!* Our Lord
Dwells not in temples made with hands. He fills
The lone heights of the everlasting hills,
And dwells with all who tremble at His word!
And I have felt His blessèd presence more,
And owned with lowlier awe its hallowing sway

On the lone hill-side or the wave-washed shore,
  Than even in His house of prayer to-day."

Then spake a third—"Oh, friends, full well I know
  The joys ye speak of; but one dearer far
Comes to me often in the ceaseless flow
  Of week-day cares, amid earth's din and jar,
When for a moment's breathing-time I pause,
  Saying, 'O Master, bless,' and lo! the while,
He stands beside me, and my spirit draws
  A heaven of rest, and gladness from His smile."

She ceased, and then one answered yet again—
  "Yea, it is *always* bliss to feel Him near
In crowd, or solitude, or sacred fane,
  But never is His presence half so dear
As when the storms of sorrow o'er us meet,
  And we with bleeding heart and baffled will,
'Faint yet pursuing' struggle to His feet,
  And lay our souls before Him, and are still."

Then all were silent, and my heart said, "Yea,
  Thou hast well spoken, thou dost well to prize,
Higher than any bliss beneath the skies,
  The faith that clings and trusts Him 'though He
    slay.'
This is the one note in the song of praise,
  Rolling from all creation round the throne,

That only human hearts sore tried can raise,
And even they in this brief life alone."

WEEP NOT FOR HER!

WEEP not for her, for she hath crossed the river,
We almost saw *Him* meet her on the shore,
And lead her through the golden gates, where never
Sorrow or death can enter any more.

Weep not for her, that she hath reached before us
The safe, warm shelter of her long-loved home;
Weep not for her, she may be bending o'er us,
In quiet wonder when we too shall come.

Weep not for her; think how she may be kneeling
Gazing her fill upon the Master's face;
A loving, humble smile, but half revealing
The perfect peace she feels in *Mary's* place.

But weep for those round whom the fight is thronging,
Who still must buckle heavy armour on,
Who dare not pray for rest, though sore their longing,
Till all the weary working day be done.

And pray for them, that they, though sad and lonely,
May still with patience bear the cross *He* sends,
And learn that tears, and wounds, and losses, only
Make peace the sweeter when the warfare ends.

AN OPEN DOOR.

OH, never say that the door is shut
To any watcher weary of sin!
Thou knowest who said, and who says it still,
" Ye weary and troubled to rest come in."
We may stand without till He says, " Too late,"
But God's is *never* a fast shut gate.

And though we have often refused to come,
And chosen to wander alone in the night,
He follows us home, and at *our* shut door
He knocks, and offers us love and light;
And He says to each, " Thou rebellious child,
I beseech thee this night to be reconciled!"

And we answer, " O Christ! it is cold and dark,
And I long to be warm, and safe, and free,
But Satan has bound me and locked the door,
And he holds me back when I touch the key
He told me once that my home was bright,
But now I feel it is always night."

And we hear a Voice, though the door is shut,
  We can catch the words though the wind is high,
As the Holy Spirit unlocks the door,
  And Jesus enters and says, "'Tis I!"
And straightway our fetters broken fall,
And we know that our Saviour has done it all.

Then never say that his door is shut—
  He loved us before we had heard his name;
He offered us pardon, and hope, and Heaven,
  And if *we* refused it, is Christ to blame?
If in unbelief we shut the gate,
Can we say that Christ has made us wait?

And He knew we were cold and hungry too,
  So He begged us to come, and be warmed, and fed,
But we passed, and knocked at another door,
  And they gave us a stone when we asked for bread;
Yet we said, "No, Lord! we will keep our sin,
Though Thy door is wide, and there's joy within."

But He waited still, though we passed Him by;
  And when all false lights had grown dim He came—
He made us willing to hear His voice,
  And 'twas He that taught us to love His name;

And He brings a light that no shade can dim,
When He dwells in us, and we in Him.

SORROWING YET ALWAYS REJOICING

NO sorrow is unmingled here,
But still, in every bitter cup
Is found the sweet ingredient, hope;
Who deepest drinks shall find it there.

Shall find it when he needs it most;
For when the night doth darkest grow,
Darkness above, all dark below,
And faith and hope are all but lost,

How oft a gleam of glory sent
Straight through the deepest, darkest night,
Has filled the soul with heavenly light,
With holy peace and sweet content!

Content to wait the will of God,
To cast on Him the heavy load,
To walk with Him the weary road
With patience, leaning on the Lord.

Content to suffer and be still,
Without complaining bear the cross,

Endure the pain, accept the loss,
Of all earth's treasures, if God will.

Content to learn by suffering long,
In darkness still to keep the faith;
Still trusting what the Saviour saith,
That perfect weakness may be strong.

Content to follow where He trod,
The Man of griefs who came to lead,
Themselves, like Him, all perfected
Through suffering, many sons to God.

Yes! there was one, and only one,
Unmingled cup of bitterness;
But God, who pitied our distress,
Gave it to His belovéd Son.

He drank it with the bitter cry,
"O Father! if it so may be,
I pray Thee let it pass from Me;
Yet be it as Thou wilt, not I."

Hadst thou, my soul, been there alone,
Thou couldst not, if, like Him oppressed,
That cup had to thy lips been pressed,
Have said with Him, "Thy will be done!"

9*

Yet from that cup all sweetness flows,
  All joy of life, all hope of heaven,
  All grace and consolation given
To sufferers in a world of woes.

Yes! and to Him who drank that cup
  In meek submission, though untold
  Its agony; who can unfold
Its sweetness now, as lifted up

Far above powers of Earth or Heaven,
  He sees the fruit His anguish bore;
  He sees the world all dead before,
Live in the life He thus hath given!

And ever as the ages glide
  His tide of joy shall onward roll,
  Till He the travail of His soul
Shall see, and shall be satisfied.

So every bitter cup of woe
  Shall yield a blessing at the last,
  And when the bitterness is past,
With living sweetness overflow.

WAITING FOR SPRING.

WAITING for Spring! The mother, watching lonely
By her sick child when all the night is dumb,
Hearing no sound save his hoarse breathing only,
Saith, "He will rally when the Spring-days come."

Waiting for Spring! Ah, me, all nature tarries
As motionless and cold she lies asleep,
Wrapt in her green pine robe that never varies,
Wearing out Winter by this southern deep.

The tints are too unbroken on the bosom
Of those great woods; we want some light-green shoots;
We want the white and red acacia blossom,
The blue life hid in all these russet roots.

Waiting for Spring! The hearts of men are watching
Each for some better, brighter, fairer thing!
Each ear a distant sound most sweet is catching,
A herald of the beauty of his spring.

Waiting for Spring! The nations in their anger
Or deadlier torpor wrapt, look onward, still

Feel a far hope through all their strife and languor,
And better spirits in them throb and thrill.

Waiting for Spring! Christians are waiting ever,
Body and soul by sin and pain bowed down;
Look for the time when all these clouds shall sever,
See high above the cross a flowery crown.

Waiting for Spring! Poor hearts! how oft ye weary
Looking for better things, and grieving much!
Earth lieth still, though all her bowers be dreary;
She trusts her God, nor thrills but at His touch.

It must be so—the man, the soul, the nation,
The mother by her child—we wait, we wait,
Dreaming out futures; life is expectation,
A grub, a root that holds our higher state.

Waiting for Spring—the germ for its perfection,
Earth for all charms by light and color given,
The body for its robe of resurrection,
Souls for their Saviour, Christians for our Heaven.

WAITING FOR CHRIST.

WE wait for Thee, all glorious One!
  We look for Thine appearing,
We bear Thy name, and on the throne
  We see Thy presence cheering.
    Faith even now
    Uplifts its brow,
And sees the Lord descending,
And with Him bliss unending.

We wait for Thee through days forlorn,
  In patient self-denial;
We know that Thou our guilt hath borne
  Upon Thy cross of trial.
    And well may we
    Submit with Thee
  To bear the cross and love it,
  Until Thy hand remove it.

We wait for Thee; already Thou
  Hast all our hearts' submission;
And though the spirit sees Thee now
  We long for open vision;
    When ours shall be
    Sweet rest with Thee
  And pure, unfading pleasure
  And life in endless measure.

We wait for Thee with certain hope—
  The time will soon be over;
With childish longing we look up
  Thy glory to discover.
      O bliss! to share
      Thy triumph there,
When home, with joy and singing
The Lord his saints is bringing.

TRUST AND REST.

FRET not, poor soul; while doubt and fear
      Disturb thy breast,
The pitying angels, who can see
How vain thy wild regret must be,
      Say, Trust and rest.

Plan not, nor scheme, but calmly wait;
      His choice is best;
While blind and erring is thy sight,
His wisdom sees and judges right,
      So trust and rest.

Strive not, nor struggle; thy poor might
      Can never wrest
The meanest thing to serve thy will;
All power is His alone; be still,
      And trust and rest.

Desire not; self-love is strong
Within thy breast;
And yet He loves thee better still,
So let Him do His loving will,
And trust and rest.

What dost thou fear? His wisdom reigns
Supreme, confessed;
His power is infinite; His love
Thy deepest, fondest dreams above,
So trust and rest.

THE HOUSE OF GOD.

ONCE slow and sad the evening fell
On desert path, on lonely dell,
As, sad and desolate,
One laid him down to sleep alone,
His couch the sand, his pillow stone,
The morning-tide to wait.

But gleamed before his dazzled sight
A radiance more than morning light,
From opened portals given;
And on his charmèd ear there rung
A sound more sweet than matin song—
The choral hymns of Heaven.

He saw the glory of that place,
Whose light is God the Saviour's face.
He saw its dwellers fair;
And learnt that— desolate, alone,
A wanderer from his Father's home,—
God's presence still was there.

So we (though often worn, oppressed,
We wander, seeking home and rest)
In sorrow's darkest hour
May see, as Jacob saw of old,
God's sunbeams bright and manifold
The shades of night o'erpower.

For not in temple hoar alone,
In cloistered shade, 'neath sculptured stone,
Stands now God's house below;
But whensoe'er His radiance bright
Gleams on our darkness and 'tis light,
His presence we may know.

Transfigured in His Glory, fair
The whole earth stands, one house of prayer—
One ante-room of Heaven;
For surely, though we know it not,
God's presence is in every spot,
To those who seek it given.

Then let us strive, and work, and wait,
As those who see that opened gate—
  That glory in our night;
So that at last, through Christ the way,
We, too, may tread that land of day,
  Where God, the Lord, is light.

THE CHILD ON THE JUDGMENT-SEAT.

WHERE hast been toiling all day, sweet-heart,
  That thy brow is burdened and sad?
The Master's work may make weary feet,
  But it leaves the spirit glad.

Was thy garden nipped with the midnight frost,
  Or scorched with the mid-day glare?
Were thy vines laid low, or thy lilies crushed,
  That thy face is so full of care?

"No pleasant garden-toils were mine!—
  I have sate on the judgment-seat,
Where the Master sits at eve and calls
  The children around His feet."

How camest thou on the judgment-seat,
  Sweet-heart? Who set thee there?
'Tis a lonely and lofty seat for thee,
  And well might fill thee with care.

"I climbed on the judgment-seat myself,
I have sate there alone all day,
For it grieved me to see the children around
Idling their life away.

"They wasted the Master's precious seed,
They wasted the precious hours;
They trained not the vines, nor gathered the fruits,
And they trampled the sweet, meek flowers."

And what hast thou done on the judgment-seat,
Sweet-heart? What didst thou there?
Would the idlers heed thy childish voice?
Did the garden mend by thy care?

"Nay, that grieved me more! I called and I cried,
But they left me there forlorn;
My voice was weak, and they heeded not,
Or they laughed my words to scorn."

Ah, the judgment-seat was not for thee!
The servants were not thine!
And the eyes which adjudge the praise and the blame,
See further than thine or mine.

The Voice that shall sound there at eve, sweet heart,
Will not raise its tones to be heard,

It will hush the earth, and hush the hearts,
And none will resist its word.

"Should I see the Master's treasures lost,
The stores that should feed His poor,
And *not* lift my voice, be it weak as it may,
And not be grievéd sore?"

Wait till the evening falls, sweet heart,
Wait till the evening falls;
The Master is near and knoweth all,
Wait till the Master calls.

But how fared thy garden-plot, sweet heart,
Whilst thou sat'st on the judgment-seat;
Who watered thy roses and trained thy vines,
And kept them from careless feet?

"Nay, that is saddest of all to me!
That is saddest of all!
My vines are trailing, my roses are parched,
My lilies droop and fall."

Go back to thy garden-plot, sweet heart!
Go back till the evening falls!
And bind thy lilies, and train thy vines,
Till for thee the Master calls.

Go make thy garden fair as thou canst,
  Thou workest never alone,
Perchance he whose plot is next to thine
  Will see it, and mend his own.

And the next may copy his, sweet heart,
  Till all grows fair and sweet,
And when the Master comes at eve,
  Happy faces His coming will greet.

Then shall thy joy be full, sweet heart,
  In the garden so fair to see,
In the Master's words of praise for all,
  In a look of His own for thee!

NOW I LAY ME DOWN TO SLEEP

IN the quiet nursery chambers,
  Snowy pillows yet unpressed,
See the forms of little children
  Kneeling, white-robed, for their rest,
All in quiet nursery chambers,
  While the dusky shadows creep,
Hear the voices of the children—
  "Now I lay me down to sleep."

In the meadow and the mountain
  Calmly shine the winter stars,
But across the glistening lowlands
  Slants the moonlight's silver bars
In the silence and the darkness,
  Darkness growing still more deep,
Listen to the little children
  Praying God their souls to keep.

"If we die"—so pray the children,
  And the mother's head drops low;
(One from out her fold is sleeping
  Deep beneath the winter's snow);
"Take our souls:" and past the casement
  Flits a gleam of crystal light,
Like the trailing of his garments,
  Walking evermore in white.

Little souls that stand expectant,
  Listen at the gates of life;
Hearing, faraway, the murmur
  Of the tumult and the strife:
We, who fight beneath those banners,
  Meeting ranks of foemen there,
Find a deeper, broader meaning
  In your simple vesper prayer.

When your hands shall grasp this standard,
  Which to-day you watch from far,

When your deeds shall shape the conflict
In this universal war,
Pray to Him, the God of battles,
Whose strong eye can never sleep,
In the warring of temptation,
Firm and true your souls to keep.

When the combat ends, and slowly
Clears the smoke from out the skies,
Then, far down the purple distance,
All the noise of battle dies.
When the last night's solemn shadows
Settle down on you and me,
May the love that never faileth
Take our souls eternally.

I.

THE LIGHT OF THE WORLD.

PAINTED BY HOLMAN HUNT.

IN the moonlight, when no murmur from the haunts of men is heard,
And the river in its sleep flows onward, onward to the sea,
And thou sleepest, who art drawing nearer to Eternity,
In the silence and the stillness comes the Word.

And He knocketh at thy portal, but thou dreamest in the night
That the flitting bat is only striking softly 'gainst the door;
Shall He knock so oft who cometh from the Heaven's eternal shore?
Sleeper in the darkness, rise, behold thy Light!

'Tis thy Priest and Prophet, clad in jewelled robe white attire;
'Tis thy King, and on His brow He wears the thorny coronal,
Budding now with amaranthine leaves and flowers ambrosial,
In His face is speaking pity, silent ire.

For His glowing lamp discloseth choking up thy dwelling door,
Deadly hemlock, barren darnel, prickly bramble, withered grasses,
And the ivy knits it closely to its stanchions and passes
Through the crevices, and hinges, and the floor.

Let Him in! for He will sojourn with the lowest and the least,
And forget that thou didst keep Him waiting in the dews and damp,

And for guerdon in the valley He will light thee
with His lamp
To the happy Shore Eternal and the Marriage
Feast.

II.

THE LIGHT OF THE WORLD.

LORD, Thou hast sought this wayward heart in
vain;
Choked by the world's vile weeds its portals
stand,
Closed to the touch of Thy redeeming Hand,
Which, knocking gently, would an entrance gain;
Oh, Love unspeakable! that Thou shouldst be
Patient amidst the night's chill falling dews,
While I Thy proffered fellowship refuse,
Slothful to rise and ope the door to Thee!
Long have I tarried, dreading yet to bear
The emblems of Thy suffering, thorns and cross
Lost in idolatry of Mammon's dross,
And lured by pleasure's transitory glare;
Henceforth vouchsafe to shed Thy light within
Illume my soul, and let these contrite tears
Blot out all record of my mis-spent years,
Dark with the sad remembrances of sin;
Then, in this purified, repentant breast,
Enter, and be for evermore my Guest!

HE LEADS US ON.

HE leads us on,
By paths we did not know,
Upward He leads us, though our steps be slow,
Though oft we faint and falter on the way,
Though storms and darkness oft obscure the day,
Yet when the clouds are gone
We know He leads us on.

He leads us on
Through all the unquiet years;
Past all our dreamland hopes, and doubts, and fears
He guides our steps. Through all the tangled maze
Of sin, of sorrow, and o'erclouded days
We know His will is done;
And still He leads us on.

And He, at last,
After the weary strife—
After the restless fever we call life—
After the dreariness, the aching pain,
The wayward struggles which have proved in vain,
After our toils are past—
Will give us rest at last.

HOLY GHOST DISPEL OUR SADNESS

HOLY GHOST, dispel our sadness,
  Pierce the clouds of sinful night;
Come, Thou source of sweetest gladness,
  Breathe Thy Life, and spread Thy Light
Loving Spirit, God of Peace!
Great Distributor of grace!
  Rest upon this congregation,
  Hear, O hear our supplication!

From that height which knows no measure,
  As a gracious shower descend
Bringing down the richest treasure
  Men can wish, or God can send!
O Thou Glory, shining down
From the Father and the Son,
  Grant us Thy illumination!
  Rest upon this congregation!

Known to Thee are all recesses
  Of the earth and spreading skies;
Every sand the shore possesses
  Thy Omniscient Mind descries.
Holy Fountain! wash us clean
Both from error and from sin!
  Make us fly what Thou refusest,
  And delight in what Thou choosest!

Manifest Thy love forever;
  Fence us in on every side;
In distress be our Reliever,
  Guard and teach, support and guide!
Let Thy kind effectual grace
Turn our feet from evil ways;
  Show Thyself our new Creator,
  And conform us to Thy nature!

Be our Friend on each occasion,
  God! omnipotent to save!
When we die, be our salvation;
  When we're buried, be our grave!
And, when from the grave we rise,
Take us up above the skies,
  Seat us with thy saints in glory,
  There forever to adore Thee!

ON AFFLICTION

AS the harp-strings only render
  All their treasures of sweet sound—
All their music, glad or tender—
  Firmly struck and tightly bound:

So the hearts of Christians owe
  Each its deepest, sweetest strain,

To the pressure firm of woe,
And the tension tight of pain

Spices crushed their pungence yield;
Trodden scents their sweets respire;
Would you have its strength revealed,
Cast the incense in the fire:

Thus the crushed and broken frame
Oft doth sweetest graces yield;
And through suffering, toil, and shame,
From the martyr's keenest flame,
Heavenly incense is distilled.

TRUST.

THE child leans on its parent's breast,
Leaves there its cares, and is at rest
The bird sits singing by its nest,
And tells aloud
His trust in God, and so is blest
'Neath every cloud.

He hath no store, he sows no seed,
Yet sings aloud, and doth not need;
By flowing streams or grassy mead,
He sings to shame
Men, who forget, in fear of need,
A Father's name.

The heart that trusts forever sings,
And feels as light as it had wings;
A well of peace within it springs;
Come good or ill,
Whate'er to-day, to-morrow brings,
It is His will!

SUBMISSION

SINCE thy Father's arm sustains thee,
Peaceful be;
When a chastening hand restrains thee,
It is He!
Know His love in full completeness,
Feel the measure of thy weakness;
If He wound thy spirit sore,
Trust Him more.

Without murmur, uncomplaining,
In His hand
Leave whatever things thou canst not
Understand;
Though the world thy folly spurneth,
From thy faith in pity turneth,
Peace thy inmost soul shall fill.
Lying still.

Like an infant, if thou thinkest
Thou canst stand,
Childlike, proudly pushing back
The proffered hand;
Courage soon is changed to fear,
Strength doth feebleness appear;
In His love if thou abide,
He will guide.

Fearest sometimes that thy Father
Hath forgot?
Though the clouds around thee gather,
Doubt Him not!
Always hath the daylight broken,
Always hath He comfort spoken;
Better hath He been for years
Than thy fears.

Therefore, whatsoe'er betideth,
Night or day,
Know His love for thee provideth
Good alway:
Crown of sorrows gladly take,
Grateful wear it, for His sake;
Sweetly bending to His will,
Lying still.

To His own thy Saviour giveth
Daily strength

To each troubled soul that liveth
Peace at length:
Weakest lambs have largest share
Of the tender Shepherd's care;
Ask Him not, then, "When?" or "How?"
Only bow!

IS THIS ALL?

SOMETIMES I catch sweet glimpses of His face,
But that is all.
Sometimes He looks on me and seems to smile,
But that is all.
Sometimes he speaks a passing word of peace,
But that is all.
Sometimes I think I hear His loving voice
Upon me call.

And is this all He meant when thus He spoke
"Come unto me?"
Is there no deeper, more enduring rest,
In Him for thee?
Is there no steadier light for thee in Him?
Oh, come and see!

Oh, come and see! oh, look, and look again!
All shall be right;
Oh, taste His love, and see that it is good,
Thou child of night.
Oh, trust Him, trust Him in his grace and power,
Then all is bright!

Nay, do not wrong Him by thy heavy thoughts,
But love His love!
Do thou full justice to His tenderness,
His mercy prove;
Take Him for what He is; oh, take Him all,
And look above!

Then shall thy tossing soul find anchorage
And steadfast peace;
Thy love shall rest on His; thy weary doubts
Forever cease.
Thy heart shall find in Him, and in His grace,
Its rest and bliss.

Christ and His love shall be thy blessèd all
For evermore!
Christ and His light shall shine on all thy ways
For evermore!
Christ and His peace shall keep thy troubled soul
For evermore!

OPEN THOU OUR EYES.

AND He drew near and talked with them,
  But they perceived Him not;
And mourned, unconscious of that light—
The gloom, the darkness, and the night,
  That wrapt His burial spot.

Wearied with doubt, perplexed and sad,
  They knew nor help, nor guide,
While He who bore the secret key
To open every mystery,
  Unknown was by their side.

Thus often when we feel alone,
  No help nor comfort near,
'Tis only that our eyes are dim;
Doubting and sad, we see not Him
  Who waiteth still to hear.

"The darkness gathers overhead,
  The morn will never come!"
Did we but raise our downcast eyes,
In the wide-flushing eastern skies
  Appears the glowing sun.

In all our daily joys and griefs
  In daily work and rest,

To those who seek Him, Christ is near,
Our bliss to calm, to soothe our care,
  In leaning on our breast.

Open our eyes, O Lord, we pray,
  To see our way, our Guide;
That by the path that here we tread,
We, following on, may still be led
  In Thy light to abide.

SHADOWS OF THE PAST.

LORD, while the shadows of the past surveying—
  And they are many since life's early morn:
Life's shadowy days have had a long delaying,
  It matters not, since they are past and gone—
                Are past and gone.

I find my steps are upward slowly tending,
  That falls the glory of thy smile upon
The golden flights of steps to heaven ascending,
  And I am journeying slowly toward the dawn—
                Toward the dawn.

I find my future in this world of sorrows
  Answers my prayers, and golden visions ope
Of providences in the bright to-morrows,
  Fulfilling prayer; this is my only hope—
                My only hope.

This pleasing hope my weary heart inspires,
  For I have prayed, and in Thy Word 'tis writ,
That they who to give Thee their warm desires,
  Shall walk the ways that they to Thee commit—
      To Thee commit.

A PRAYER FOR YOU.

I HAVE a Saviour—He's pleading in glory—
  So precious, though earthly enjoyments be few;
And now He's watching in tenderness o'er me;
  But, oh, that my Saviour was your Saviour too!
  For you I am praying—I'm praying for you!

I have a Father—to me He has given
  A hope for eternity, precious and true;
And soon will my spirit be with Him in heaven;
  But, oh, that He'd let me bring you with me too!
  For you I am praying—I'm praying for you!

I have a Crown, and I'll wear it forever,
  Encircled with jewels of heavenly hue;
'Twas purchased by Jesus, my glorified Saviour;
  But, oh, could I know one was purchased for you!
  For you I am praying—I'm praying for you!

I have a Robe—'tis resplendent in whiteness—
  Awaiting in glory my wondering view:
Oh, when I'll receive it, all shining in brightness,

Dear friend, could I see you receiving one too!
For you I am praying—I'm praying for you!

I have a Rest—and the earnest is given—
Though now, for a time, 'tis concealed from my view;
This life everlasting, 'tis Jesus, 'tis heaven;
And, oh, dearest friend, let me meet you there too!
For you I am praying—I'm praying for you!

I have a Peace, and it's calm as a river—
A peace that the friend of the world never knew;
My Saviour alone is its Author and Giver;
But, oh, could I know it was given to you!
For you I am praying—I'm praying for you!

For you I am praying—for you I am praying!
For you I am praying—for you, yes, for you!
And soon shall I hear you rejoicing and saying:
"Your dear, loving Saviour is my Saviour too!"
And prayer will be answered for you—yes, for you!

And when He has found you, tell others the story,
How Jesus extended His mercy to you;
Then point them away to the regions of glory,

And pray that your Saviour may bring them
 there too!
 For prayer will be answered—'twas answered
 for you!

Oh, speak of that Saviour, that Father in heaven;
 That Harp, Crown, and Robe which are waiting
 for you!
That Peace you possess, and that Rest to be given!
 Still praying that Jesus may save them like you;
 And prayer will be answered—'twas answered
 for you!

HEAR MY CRY!

O STRONG to save and bless,
My rock and righteousness
 Draw near to me!
Blessing, and joy, and might,
Wisdom, and love, and light
 Are all with Thee!

My refuge and my rest,
As child on mother's breast,
 I lean on Thee!
From faintness and from fear.
When foes and ill are near,
 Deliver me!

Turn not away Thy face,
Withhold not needed grace,
My fortress be!
Perils are round and round
Iniquities abound—
See, Saviour, see!

Come, God and Saviour, come!
I can no more be dumb;
Appeal I must
To Thee, the Gracious One,
Else is my hope all gone,
I sink in dust!

Oh, answer me, my God,
Thy love is deep and broad,
Thy grace is true!
Thousands this grace have shared
Oh, let me *now* be heard,
Oh, love *me* too!

Descend Thou mighty love,
Descend from heaven above,
Fill Thou this soul!
Heal every bruiséd part,
Bind up this broken heart,
And make me whole.

'Tis knowing Thee that heals;
'Tis seeing Thee that seals
Comfort and peace!
Show me Thy cross and blood,
My Saviour and my God,
Then troubles cease.

FRUITLESS TOIL.

"LORD, I have toiled all night,
And still unbless'd my hand;
Yet I will launch into the deep
Once more at Thy command.

"I hear triumphant songs
Swell from the banks around,
Each answering each with joyful cry
But *I* no spoil have found.

"Fruitless is all my toil,
Through long night-watches past,
My heart is sick with hope deferred;
But Thou art come at last."

The fisher's hands hung down;
Dull was his heart, and faint,
When a heavenly voice the silence broke,
And answered his complaint.

"When have I left thee, son,
That thou shouldst droop with fear?
When hast thou sought my sympathy
And hast not found Me near?

"Not fruitless is thy toil,
If thou my cross wouldst bear·
I do but ask thy willing heart
To grave my image there.

"For each net vainly cast
Stronger thine arm will prove;
The trial of thy patient hope
Is witness of Thy love.

"The time, the place, the way
Are open to mine eye;
I sent thee—not to gather spoil—
To labor patiently.

"My son! was not thy cry,
'Increase my faith, O Lord!
More of Thyself, and more like Thee
Behold, thy prayer is heard.

"Oh, trust Me with thy crown,
'Tis hidden safe with Me;
A little while, and where I am,
There shall my servant be.

"Bright seems thy brother's lot;
  But, child, is *thine* so dim?
The King, thy Friend, hath asked of thee
  To watch one hour with HIM!"

THE TWO WORLDS.

TWO worlds there are. To one our eyes we strain,
Whose magic joys we shall not see again;
  Bright haze of morning veils its glimmering shore;
    Ah, truly breathed we there
    Intoxicating air—
  Glad were our hearts in that sweet realm of Nevermore.

The lover there drank her delicious breath,
Whose love has yielded since to change or death;
  The mother kissed her child whose days are o'er.
    Alas! too soon have fled
    The irreclaimable dead:
  We see them—visions strange—amid the Nevermore.

The merry song some maiden used to sing—
The brown, brown hair that once was wont to cling

To temples long clay-cold: to the very core
They strike our weary hearts,
As some vexed memory starts
From that long faded land—the realm of
Nevermore.

It is perpetual summer there. But here
Sadly we may remember rivers clear,
And harebells quivering on the meadow-floor,
For brighter bells and bluer,
For tenderer hearts and truer,
People that happy land—the realm of
Nevermore.

Upon the frontier of this shadowy land
We pilgrims of eternal sorrow stand:
What realm lies forward, with its happier store
Of forests green and deep,
Of valleys hushed in sleep,
And lakes most peaceful? 'Tis the land of
Evermore.

Very far off its marble cities seem—
Very far off—beyond our sensual dream—
Its woods, unruffled by the wild winds' roar:
Yet does the turbulent surge
Howl on its very verge.
One moment—and we breathe within the
Evermore.

They whom we loved and lost so long ago,
Dwell in those cities, far from mortal woe—
  Haunt those fresh woodlands, whence sweet
      carolings soar.
    Eternal peace have they:
    God wipes their tears away:
  They drink that river of life which flows for
    Evermore.

Thither we hasten through these regions dim,
But lo! the white wings of the Seraphim
  Shine in the sunset! On that joyous shore
    Our lightened hearts shall know
    The life of long ago:
  The sorrow-burdened past shall fade for
    Evermore

THE TWO ANGELS.

TWO angels, one of Life and one of Death,
  Passed o'er our village as the morning broke;
The dawn was on their faces, and beneath
  The sombre houses hearsed with plumes of
    smoke.

Their attitude and aspect were the same;
  Alike their features, and their robes of white;

But one was crowned with amaranth, as with flame,
  And one with asphodels, like flakes of light.

I saw them pause on their celestial way;
  Then said I, with deep fear and doubt oppressed,
"Beat not so loud, my heart, lest thou betray
  The place where thy belovéd are at rest!"

And he who wore the crown of asphodels,
  Descending at my door, began to knock;
And my soul sank within me, as in wells
  The waters sink before an earthquake's shock.

I recognized the nameless agony,
  The terror, and the tremor, and the pain,
That oft before had filled or haunted me,
  And now returned with threefold strength again.

The door I opened to my heavenly guest,
  And listened, for I thought I heard God's voice;
And, knowing whatsoe'r He sent was best,
  Dared neither to lament nor to rejoice.

Then with a smile, that filled the house with light,
  "My errand is not Death, but Life," he said;
And, ere I answered, passing out of sight,
  On his celestial embassy he sped.

Twas at thy door, O friend! and not at mine
  The angel with the amaranthine wreath,
Pausing, descended, and with voice divine,
  Whispered a word that had a sound like Death.

Then fell upon the house a sudden gloom,
  A shadow on those features fair and thin;
And softly from that hushed and darkened room
  Two angels issued, where but one went in.

All is of God! If He but wave His hand,
  The mists collect, the rain falls thick and loud,
Till, with a smile of light on sea and land,
  Lo! He looks back from the departing cloud.

Angels of life and death alike are His;
  Without His leave they pass no threshold o'er
Who, then, would wish or dare, believing this,
  Against His messengers to shut the door?

IS THERE NO BALM IN GILEAD?

IS there no balm in Gilead, then? is there no
  Healer nigh?
No freshening spring to cheer the waste so deso-
  late and dry?
Hath Hope's dear vision vanished forever from
  thy sight,

And darkness fallen around thee, the very gloom
of night?
And seems thy soul forsaken, her every blessing
flown?
No soothing for her sorrow, and nowhere to make
her moan?
Yet stay; the cross thou bearest thus hath first
been borne for thee,
Jesus Himself did hang thereon, thy life and cure
to be.

For thine own ease He bare it all,—the scourge
and piercing thorn,
The nailing and the bruising, the denial, shame,
and scorn;
Darkness and desolation deep, and pangs beyond
thy thought,
And all for thy soul's healing these sad agonies
were wrought.
Upon His Cross He yearned for thee, for thee His
heartstrings brake;
Himself of all forsaken, He could not thee forsake;
Then evermore, when chastenings sore thine inmost
spirit wring,
Say, My Belov'd is crucified, and I to Him will cling.

How shall I sing Thy holy love, dear Passion of
my Lord?
Or how Thy mystic virtue shall I worthily record?

Thou art the spring of all our hope, the balsam
of our woes,
The solace of our yearnings, and the bower of
our repose,
True Paradise of all delights, since joy of grief
is born;
For, as the flowers but close at night to ope more
fresh with morn,
So He who wept and bled for us, and bowed in
earthly gloom,
Now makes those sorrows our bright bliss, those
wounds our joyous home.

Here is a covert from the storm, when winds and
waves arise,
A shadow in the scorching noon, a light in star-
less skies;
A staff upon the rugged road, a shield when foes
assail,
A charm Divine, against whose might no evil can
prevail;
For where the Cross of Jesus is, is peace, and
there alone,
And 'neath that banner of His love He gathereth
His own;
And those who will be Christ's must not e'er
grudge their portion small,
Who in His bitter chalice, once, and for thee,
drained it all.

Thou know'st He went not up to joy, but first
He suffered pain,
And all the self-same path must tread who thus
His bliss would gain:
Is aught too wearisome or hard for Jesus' sake to
bear?
While He is crowned with thorns wilt thou a
crown of roses wear?
Lo! this good Cross He offers thee; it is thy very
life;
Anoint with holy unction, it will aid thee in the
strife;
'Tis hallowed by thy Saviour's touch, who hung
on it for thee,
And Love's sweet night shall make it light, and
win the victory.

Draw near, thou reft and drooping heart, draw
near and lift thy gaze
To Him who yearns with outstretched arms thee
from thy grief to raise;
Draw near, and, clinging close beneath thy Sa-
viour's bleeding heart,
Tell o'er each throb of that deep woe in which
thou hast a part;
Tell o'er each drop of dear life-blood which ebbs
for thee so fast,
And all thy weary heart-aching upon that true
love cast·

In Jesus' Cross and Passion is the medicine of thy
soul,
Yea, there is balm in Gilead, and a Healer to make
thee whole.

CHRIST'S CALL TO THE SOUL.

FAIR soul, created in the primal hour,
Once pure and grand,
And for whose sake I left My throne and power
At God's right hand;
By this sad heart pierced through because I loved
thee;
Let love and mercy to contrition move thee.

Cast off the sins thy holy beauty veiling,
Spirit divine!
Vain against thee the hosts of hell assailing,
My strength is thine!
Drink from My side the cup of life immortal,
And love shall lead the path to heaven's portal.

I for thy sake was pierced with many sorrows,
And bore the cross,
Yet heeded not the galling of the arrows,
The shame and loss.
So faint not, then, whate'er the burden be,
But bear it bravely, even to Calvary.

THEIR NAMES.

SWEET thought, my God! that on the palms
  Of Thy most holy hands
Are graven all Thy peoples' names,
  Though countless as the sands.

Not one too mean to have his place
  Amid that record blest,
And if but there our names are found,
  We'll share the heavenly rest.

How can we then yield to distrust,
  Or think we are forgot,
While ever thus the care of One
  Who loves and changes not?

TWO

TWO buds plucked from the tree,
  Two birdies flown from the nest,
Two little darlings snatched
  From a fond mother's breast.
Two little snow-white lambs
  Gone from the sheltering fold,
Two little narrow graves
  Down in the graveyard cold.

Two little drooping flowers
  Growing in purer air,
Blooming fragrant and bright
  In the Gardener's care.
Two little tender birds
  Flown far from fear and harm,
Two little snow-white lambs
  In the Good Shepherd's arm.

Two little angels more
  Singing with voices sweet,
Flinging their crowns of gold
  Down at their Saviour's feet.
Free from all earthly care,
  Pure from all earthly stain,
Oh, who could wish them back
  In this drear world again?

*"HIS TRUTH SHALL BE THY SHIELD AND BUCKLER."**

When my sins in aspect dread
  Meet like waters o'er my head,
Seen in light of God's own face,
Darker for his offered grace—
When I sigh for healing rest,
By a hopeless yoke opprest,

* Psalms xci. 4.

Struggling in a grasp too strong,
Borne as by a wind along—
Then, I hear that Voice from Heaven,
"Knock, and entrance shall be given—
Him that comes, whoe'er he be,
I will never cast from Me!"
When *I* come, with trembling heart,
Will the Saviour say, "Depart?"
Shall I find His pardon free
Is in wrath denied to *me?*
Is my guilt so deep in stain
That the cleansing blood is vain?
"Heaven and earth shall pass away,
Not My Words—" so Christ doth say:
In that hour, "His Truth shall be
Shield and buckler unto thee."

When the clouds have hid His face,
And His path no more I trace,
And all comforts that illume
Life, have faded into gloom—
Quenched each earth-enkindled spark,
Can I trust Him in the dark?
Will my wavering faith still hold
To a promise breathed of old?
When I meet some foe unknown,
Shall I find myself alone?
Soul, by *faith* thou walkest here:

Though nor sun nor stars appear,
Wait and watch throughout the night,
And till daybreak ask not *sight!*
All unseen, thy Heavenly Guide
Walks, through darkness, at thy side.
"Heaven and earth shall pass away,
NOT MY WORDS—" so Christ doth say:
In the gloom "HIS TRUTH shall be
Shield and buckler unto thee."

In the terrors of the night,
In the mid-day arrows' flight,
When destruction wasteth near,
And all faces blanch with fear,
When a thousand round me fall,
Shall I trust Thee calm through all?
Will this trembling spirit be
Kept "in perfect peace" by Thee?
Though all stable things may end,
Earth and sky in tempest blend,
Shall I lean upon Thy breast,
And beneath Thy shadow rest?
Wilt Thou arm my soul with power.
Ne'er experienced till that hour?
"Heaven and earth shall pass away,
NOT MY WORDS—" so Christ doth say
In that strait "HIS TRUTH shall be
Shield and buckler unto thee."

As the weary years go by,
Will my love wax cold, and die?
If the pilgrimage be long,
Life be dark, and foes be strong,
Shall I not grow faint, and yield?
Shall I ever win the field?
How shall I endure and dare?
How the cross in patience bear?
How through tedious years sustain
Wavering conflict, oft in vain?
Nay, but the Unchanging Friend
"Will confirm you *to the end!*"
"He Who hath the work begun
Ne'er will leave that work undone—"
While at God's right hand He lives,
Deathless is the life He gives,
Through all change, and woe, and strife,
"Springing up to endless Life."
"Heaven and earth shall pass away,
Not My Words—" so Christ doth say:
In all years "His Truth shall be
Shield and buckler unto thee."

When I reach life's earthly bound,
And the shadows darken round,
All familiar things and dear
Fading fast from eye and ear,—
In that hour of mortal smart,

Trembling flesh and failing heart,
Shall I find my anchor vain,
Parting in that latest strain?
Hear the Shepherd's voice of old,
Looking on His helpless fold,
Looking far, with gaze Divine,
Down the ages' lengthening line.
"Every feeble sheep I know:
Life eternal I bestow:
None shall pluck them from My hand."
Shall that word of promise stand?
Or, when countless foes affright,
Closing round in latest fight,
In that deadly hour and dim,
Shall my soul be snatched from HIM?
"Heaven and earth shall pass away,
NOT MY WORDS—" so Christ doth say:
In death's grasp "His TRUTH shall be
Shield and buckler unto thee."

THE OTHER SIDE.

WE dwell this side of Jordan's stream,
Yet oft there comes a shining beam
Across from yonder shore;
While visions of a holy throng,
And sound of harp, and seraph song,
Seem gently wafted o'er.

The other side! Ah, there's the place
Where saints in joy past times retrace,
And think of trials gone;
The veil withdrawn, they clearly see
That all on earth had need to be,
To bring them safely home.

The other side! No sin is there,
To stain the robes that blessed ones wear
Made white in Jesus' blood:
No cry of grief, no voice of woe,
To mar the peace their spirits know--
Their constant peace with God.

The other side! Its shore so bright
Is radiant with the golden light
Of Zion's city fair!
And many dear ones gone before
Already tread the happy shore:
I seem to see them there.

The other side! Oh, charming sight!
Upon its banks, arrayed in white,
For me a loved one waits:
Over the stream he calls to me,
Fear not—I am thy guide to be,
Up to the pearly gates.

The other side! His well-known voice,
And dear, bright face, will me rejoice:
We'll meet in fond embrace.
He'll lead me on, until we stand,
Each with a palm-branch in our hand,
Before the Saviour's face.

The other side! The other side!
Who would not brave the swelling tide
Of earthly toil and care;
To wake one day, when life is past,
Over the stream, at home at last,
With all the blessed ones there!

I AM CHRIST'S, AND CHRIST IS MINE.

LONG did I toil, and knew no earthly rest;
Far did I rove, and found no certain home
At last I sought them in His sheltering breast
Who opes His arms, and bids the weary come.
With Him I found a home, a rest divine;
And I since then am His, and He is mine.

Yes, He is mine! and naught of earthly things,
Not all the charms of pleasure, wealth, or power
The fame of heroes, or the pomp of kings,
Could tempt me to forego His love an hour:
Go, worthless world, I cry, with all that's thine!
Go! I my Saviour's am, and He is mine.

The good I have is from His stores supplied;
  The ill is only what He deems the best;
He for my friend, I'm rich with naught beside,
  And poor without Him, though of all possest;
Changes may come; I take, or I resign;
Content while I am His, while He is mine.

Whate'er may change, in Him no change is seen;
  A glorious sun, that wanes not nor declines;
Above the clouds and storms He walks serene,
  And sweetly on His peoples' darkness shines:
All may depart; I fret not, nor repine,
While I my Saviour's am, while He is mine.

He stays me falling, lifts me up when down,
  Reclaims me wandering, guards from every foe,
Plants on my worthless brow the victor's crown,
  Which, in return, before His feet I throw;
Grieved that I cannot better grace His shrine
Who deigns to own me His, as He is mine.

While here, alas! I know but half His love,
  But half discern Him, and but half adore;
But when I meet Him in the realms above,
  I hope to love Him better, praise Him more;
And feel, and tell, amid the choir divine,
How fully I am His, and He is mine.

SATISFIED.

O JESUS! Friend unfailing,
How dear art Thou to me!
Are cares or fears assailing?
I find my strength in Thee!
Why should my feet grow weary
Of this my pilgrim way?
Rough though the path, and dreary,
It ends in perfect day.

Naught, naught I count as treasure,
Compared, O Christ, with Thee!
Thy sorrow without measure
Earned peace and joy for me.
I love to own, Lord Jesus!
Thy claims o'er me and mine:
Bought with Thy blood most precious,
Whose can I be but Thine?

What fills my soul with gladness?
'Tis Thine abounding grace!
Where can I look in sadness,
But, Jesus, on Thy face?
My all is Thy providing;
Thy love can ne'er grow cold;
In Thee, my Refuge, hiding,
No good wilt Thou withhold!

Why should I droop in sorrow?
  Thou'rt ever by my side:
Why, trembling, dread the morrow?
  What ill can e'er betide?
If I my Cross have taken,
  'Tis but to follow Thee;
If scorned, despised, forsaken,
  Naught severs Thee from me!

Oh, worldly pomp and glory!
  Your charms are spread in vain!
I've heard a sweeter story,
  I've found a truer gain!
Where Christ a place prepareth,
  There is my loved abode;
There shall I gaze on Jesus,
  There shall I dwell with God!

For every tribulation,
  For every sore distress,
In Christ I've full salvation,
  Sure help, and quiet rest.
No fear of foes prevailing!
  I triumph, Lord, in Thee!
O Jesus! Friend unfailing!
  How dear art Thou to me!

THE DAY OF REST.

O DAY most calm, most bright,
The fruit of this, the next world's bud
The endorsement of supreme delight,
Writ by a Friend, and with His blood;
The couch of time, care's balm and bay:
The week were dark but for Thy light,
Thy torch doth show the way.

The other days and thou
Make up one man, whose face Thou art,
Knocking at Heaven with thy brow;
The worky-days are the back part;
The burden of the week lies there,
Making the whole to stoop and bow,
Till thy release appear.

Man had straightforward gone
To endless death; but thou dost pull
And turn us round to look on One,
Whom, if we were not very dull,
We could not choose but look on still
Since there is no place so alone,
The which He doth not fill.

Sundays the pillars are
On which Heaven's palace archéd lies;

The other days fill up the spare
And hollow room, with vanities.
They are the fruitful beds and borders,
In God's rich garden, that is bare,
Which parts their ranks and orders.

The Sundays of man's life,
Threaded together on time's string,
Make bracelets to adorn the wife
Of the eternal, glorious King.
On Sunday Heaven's gate stands ope;
Blessings are plentiful and rife—
More plentiful than hope.

This day my Saviour rose,
And did enclose this light for His;
That, as each beast His manger knows,
Man might not of his fodder miss.
Christ hath took in this piece of ground,
And made a garden there for those
Who want herbs for their wound.

The rest of our creation
Our great Redeemer did remove,
With the same shake, which at His Passion
Did the earth and all things with it move.
As Samson bore the doors away,
Christ's hands, though nailed, wrought our salvation,
And did unhinge that day.

The brightness of that day
We sullied by our foul offence;
Wherefore that robe we cast away,
Having a new at His expense.
Whose drops of blood paid the full price
That was required to make us gay,
And fit for Paradise.

Thou art a day of mirth;
And where the week-days trail on ground,
Thy flight is higher, as thy birth;
O let me take thee at the bound,
Groping with thee from seven to seven,
Till that we both, being tossed from earth,
Fly hand in hand to Heaven!

THE SHULAMITE AT THE LORD'S FEET

POOR heart! why throb thus wildly in my breast?
The more I ponder on my Master's word,
The more are doubts and fears within me stirr'd,
Long as my eyes on my own weakness rest.

I to come forth! What, I! 'Twas so He said—
My wav'ring steps to others must be guide,
My feeble arm must 'gainst the foe be tried;
There a whole world—and here a lowly maid!

Ah, no, my Lord! and yet the call is Thine!
  I spoke unwisely, keeping self in sight;
  I'll only look on Thy all-saving might—
Be calm, my heart! for my Beloved is mine.

Yes, my Beloved is mine—what wouldst thou more?
  The cause is His! It is His work I do!
  He is my rock, my shield and buckler too;
Of strength and wisdom my unfailing store.

And I am His. Oh, heart, be faithful still!
  Still let Him lead me as it seems Him best!
  With Him to combat, or with Him to rest,
March, or encamp, according to His will.

My Friend is mine, and I forever His:
  Himself he gave, myself to Him I give;
  In me He dwells—in Him alone I live:
Was ever union half so blest as this?

THE LOVE THAT PASSETH KNOWLEDGE

NOT what I am, O Lord, but what Thou art!
  That, that alone can be my soul's true rest;
Thy love, not mine, bids fear and doubt depart,
  And stills the tempest of my tossing breast.

It is Thy perfect love that casts out fear;
I know the voice that speaks the "It is I;"
And in these well-known words of heavenly cheer,
I hear the joy that bids each sorrow fly.

Thy name is Love! I hear it from yon Cross;
Thy name is Love! I read it in yon tomb;
All meaner love is perishable dross,
But this shall light me through time's thickest gloom.

It blesses now, and shall forever bless;
It saves me now, and shall forever save;
It holds me up in days of helplessness,
It bears me safely o'er each swelling wave.

Girt with the love of God on every side,
Breathing that love as Heaven's own healing air,
I work or wait, still following my guide,
Braving each foe, escaping every snare.

'Tis what I know of Thee, my Lord and God,
That fills my soul with peace, my lips with song;
Thou art my health, my joy, my staff and rod;
Leaning on Thee, in weakness I am strong.

I am all want and hunger; this faint heart
Pines for a fullness which it finds not here,
Dear ones are leaving, and, as they depart,
Make room within for something yet more dear.

More of Thyself, oh, show me hour by hour
  More of thy glory, O my God and Lord!
More of Thyself in all Thy grace and power,
  More of Thy love and truth, Incarnate Word!

THE SHEEP-TRACK.

TWO ways: only two. One leadeth
    Home to the land of rest,
And the Good Shepherd guides the flock He
        feedeth,
    The road He knoweth best.

The feeble lamb, within His bosom hiding,
    Is precious as the strong;
The sick He tends: in sweet compassion guiding
    The weary one with young.

He leads them forth, He goeth out before them;
    And where the two ways meet,
They look to Him, whose eye is watching o'er them.
    To guide their wavering feet.

They own a mark by which the Master claims them,
    Though oft the sign seems dim;
And well they know the Shepherd King who
        names them—
    They hear and follow Him.

Sweet sounds His voice. All other calls unheeding,
They watch where He may lead;
And in His face of love His wishes reading,
The flock that track will tread.

Narrow it is, and rough, and often lonely,
Upon the mountain steep:
There's room for Jesus, and for Jesus only
And for His timid sheep.

Around spread flowery fields where in their blindness
The careless ones would roam:
Sharp seems the Shepherd's rod that falls in kindness
To bring the wanderers home.

Fierce howls the wolf, and adders creep around them;
But succor He will send;
For He who in the wilderness first found them
Will keep them to the end.

Two ways: only two. The other bendeth
Down unto hell beneath!
Broad is the gate, and frantic mirth ascendeth
From crowds that rush to death.

No heavenly friend will soothe their hopeles sorrow,
No arm their burden bear;
No fold of rest awaits them on the morrow,
No Shepherd King is there.

For *them* death's bondage, and a night of weeping
That hath no dawn of day.
Oh, Christ! who o'er Thy flock Thy watch art keeping,
Thou art the Truth, the Way!

'IN ALL TIME OF OUR TRIBULATION GOOD LORD, DELIVER US!"

SAVIOUR! by Thy sweet compassion,
So unmeasured, so Divine;
By that bitter, bitter Passion;
By that crimson Cross of Thine;
By the woes Thy love once tasted
In this sin-marred world below,
Succor those in tribulation,
Succor those in sorrow now.

Thou Who wast so sorely burdened,
Help the weak that are oppressed;
Sanctify all earthly crosses,
For the coming day of rest;

Give the meek a trustful spirit
  That will always lean on Thee,
And in storms of deep affliction
  Still Thy gracious Presence see.

Lord, Thou hast a holy purpose
  In each suffering we bear;
In each throe of pain and terror,
  In each secret, silent tear;
In the weary days of sickness,
  Famine, want, and loneliness;
In our night-time of bereavement,
  In our soul's Lent-bitterness.

All the needful sweet correction
  Of this gentle Hand of Thine,
All Thy wise and careful nurture,
  All Thy faultless discipline:
All to purge the precious metal,
  Till it will reflect Thy face;
All to shape and polish jewels
  Thine Own diadem to grace.

Lord, we know that we must ever
  Take our cross and follow Thee
All along the narrow pathway,
  If we would Thy glory see.

Then, oh, help us each to bear it,
  By Thine own hard life of shame;
Let us suffer well and meekly,
  Let us glorify Thy name.

Cheer the weak ones who are bending
  'Neath this weary burden now;
Lift the pallid faces upward,
  Smooth the care-worn, furrowed brow;
Send a bright and hopeful message
  To each tried and tempted heart,
That the thick and gloomy shadows
  At that sunshine may depart.

Tell them Thou canst see all sorrow
  In this world's rough wilderness;
Tell them Thou art near to succor,
  Near to comfort and to bless;
Tell them of Thy Cross and Passion,
  Tell them of Thy trials sore,
Tell them of the Angel-city
  Where is joy for evermore.

VISITATION OF THE SICK.

PEACE to this house! O Thou Whose way
Was on the waves, Whose voice did stay
The wild wind's rage, come, Lord, and say,
Peace to this house!

Thou, Who in pity for the weak
Didst quit Thy heavenly Throne to seek
And save the lost, come, Lord, and speak
Peace to this house!

Thou, Who dost all our sorrows know
And when our tears of anguish flow
Dost feel compassion, come, bestow
Peace on this house!

Thou, Who in agony didst pray,
"Take, Father, take this cup away,"
And then wast strengthened, come and say,
Peace to this house!

O Conqueror by suffering!
O mighty Victor! glorious King!
From out of pain and sorrow bring
Peace to this house!

Thou, Who triumphant from the dead
Thine Hands didst o'er the Apostles spread
And say, "Peace to you," come, and shed
Peace on this house!

Thou, Who didst on the clouds ascend
And then the Holy Spirit send,
Send Him to comfort, and defend
All in this house!

Lord, in the Sacramental food
Of Thine own Body and Thy Blood,
Peace that is felt, not understood,
Give to this house!

Save, save us sinking in the deep,
Give ease from pain and quiet sleep,
And under Thy wing's shelter keep
All in this house!

"Peace to this house," come, Lord, and say
Come to us, Lord, and with us stay,
Oh, give, and never take away
Peace from this house!

And when at last our fainting breath
On trembling lips scarce quivereth,
Oh, bring us through the gate of Death,
Lord, to Thine House!

To Thine own House in Paradise,
To Thine own House above the sk.es,
To live the life that never dies,
Lord, in Thine House!

THE MYSTERY OF CHRIST.

I MARVEL night and day, and cannot cease—
Ask evermore, Can this thing be?
Heaven brought to earth—her Maker made my peace,
God bound, to set me free!

I cannot love Thee as I would and ought;
But, by Thy grace presenting still,
From all things else to Thee returns my thought,
And brings Thee back my will.

All thoughts, all searches, to this centre tend;
All rays in this one focus meet;
Here, as of old, the wise men journeying send
Their treasures at Thy feet.

There is no record, but doth hint of Thee;
All history else were false and vain;
The stones Thy kingdom preach; loosed with this key,
All hardest things are plain.

There is no wisdom but doth taste of Thine;
  All lights that did Thine own forerun
Caught Thy prevenient gleams, as clouds that shine
  In the unrisen sun.

The glories of earth's empires, age by age
  Submitting grandly to decay,
Were but the' illusive dawn that did presage
  Thy fixed and perfect day.

Art's beauteous dreams, the charm of thought and song,
  The majesty of rule and law,
The single mind outsoaring from the throng,
  Gifted a world to draw,--

What were they all but preludes poor and faint
  Of Thy supreme imperial reign
In glory and in beauty, when each saint
  Thy likeness shall attain?

Thou hast been here; of old, as now,
  Walking unseen the paths we go;
But in the central years, one lifetime, Thou
  Thy visible form didst show.

A cloud did steal Thee from us; but that hour
  Thy glorious ministry began;
Thou gav'st the word—from thence, with quickening power,
  That word the earth o'erran.

Thou art not gone, but hidden; to our sense
  Thou shalt return; Thou didst not show
Thy glory at the first, whose height immense
  Stooped to our stature low.

Till Thy true advent dawn, Thy Church, like Thee,
  Shall suffer, die, and rise again;
Then, glorified, made white, eternally
  With Thee on earth shall reign.

THE GIVER AND THE GIFTS

THE path I trod so pleasant was and fair,
  I counted it life's best;
Forgetting that Thou, Lord, hadst placed me there
  To journey towards Thy rest.

Forgetting that the path was only good
  Because the homeward way,
I held it fullest beauty where I stood—
  I thought these gleams the day.

I know I might have seen in every star
That sheds its light on me,
A lamp of Thine, set out to guide from far
My steps towards home and Thee;—

Have heard in streams with bending grasses clad
Which sparkled through the sod,
The music of the river that makes glad
The city of our God;—

In flowers plucked but to wither in my hand,
Or passed with lingering feet,
Have read my Father's promise of a land
Where flowers are still more sweet.

And I have knelt, how often, thanking Thee
For what Thy love hath given,
Then turned away to bend to these my knee,
And seek in these my Heaven.

Forgive me that I, looking for the day,
Forget whence it would shine;
And turned Thy helps to reasons for delay,
And loved not Thee, but Thine.

Yet most for the cold heart with which I write
Of sin so faintly felt:—
This frost of doubt, this darkness as of night
Thy love can cheer and melt.

On me unworthy shed, O Lord, the glow
Of Thy dear light and love,
That I may walk with trusting faith below,
Towards the fair land above;

That I may learn in all Thy gifts to see
The love that on me smiled,
And find in all I have a thought of Thee,
Who thus hast blessed Thy child;

And most in what Thy tenderest love hath given
Those to my heart most dear;
May I through these look upward to Thy Heaven,
In these find Thee most near.

"I WILL ARISE AND GO TO MY FATHER."

I ASK if Thou canst love me still, O God?
They say Thou canst not love so weak a thing—
One that was angered by a Father's rod,
One that hath wayward and rebellious been,
Unstable, thankless, prone to every sin.
Thou knowest all—yet whither shall I go,
To leave my sins and with them leave my woe,
Except to Thee, who only help canst bring,
And bid me live thy pardoning love to sing?

I come, my sinful thoughts have vexed me long;
I fly, for evil spirits round me throng,
And I am weak, but Thou, my God, art strong!
My tears are flowing—no, Thou canst not see
Thy child in anguish and not pity me.
I lay my head upon thy infinite heart,
I hide beneath the shelter of thy wing;
Pursued, and tempted, helpless, I must cling
To Thee, my Father; bid me not depart,
For sin and death pursue, and life is where Thou art!

WAKING.

I HAVE done, at length, with dreaming;
  Henceforth, O Thou Soul of mine,
Thou must take up sword and gauntlet,
  Waging warfare most divine.
Life is struggle, combat, victory—
  Wherefore have I slumbered on
With my forces all unmarshaled,
  With my weapons all undrawn?
Oh, how many a glorious record
  Had the angel of me kept,
Had I done instead of doubted,
  Had I warred instead of wept!

But, begone! regret, bewailing,
  Ye but weaken at the best;
I have tried the trusty weapons
  Resting erst within my breast:
I have wakened to my duty,
  To a knowledge strong and deep,
That I dreamed not of aforetime
  In my long, inglorious sleep:
For to lose is something awful,
  And I knew it not before;
And I dreamed not how stupendous
  Was the secret that I bore—
The great, deep, mysterious secret
  Of a life to be wrought out
Into warm, heroic action,
  Weakened not by fear or doubt.
In this subtle sense of living,
  Newly stirred in every vein,
I can feel a throb electric,
  Pleasure half-allied to pain.—
'Tis so great—and yet so awful—
  So bewildering, yet so brave,
To be king in every conflict
  Where before I crouched a slave.
It's so glorious to be conscious
  Of a glorious power within,
Stronger than the rallying forces
  Of a charged and marshaled sin.

Never in those old romances
  Felt I half the sense of life
That I feel within me stirring
  Standing in the place of strife.
Oh, those olden days of dalliance,
  When I wantoned with my fate,
When I trifled with a knowledge
  That well-nigh had come too late
Yet, my Soul, look not behind thee,
  Thou hast work to do at last;
Let the brave toil of the Present
  Overarch the crumbling Past;
Build thy great acts high, and higher
  Build them on the conquered sod
Where thy weakness first fell bleeding,
  And thy first prayer rose to God.

NOTHING BUT LEAVES.

NOTHING but leaves: the spirit grieves
  Over a wasted life.
Sins committed while conscience slept;
Promises made, but never kept;
  Hatred, battle, and strife—
      Nothing but leaves.

Nothing but leaves: no garnered sheaves
  Of life's fair ripened grain;

Words, idle words, for earnest deeds.
We sow our seed—lo! tares and weeds
Go reap with toil and pain
Nothing but leaves.

Nothing but leaves: memory weaves
No veil to sever the past;
As we return our weary way,
Counting each lost and misspent day,
We find sadly, at last,
Nothing but leaves.

And shall we meet the Master so,
Bearing our withered leaves?
The Saviour looks for perfect fruit:
We stand before Him, humbled, mute,
Waiting the word He breathes—
Nothing but leaves.

PAUL GERHARDT'S HYMN

COMETH sunshine after rain,
After morning joy again;
After heavy, bitter grief,
Dawneth surely sweet relief:
And my soul, who, from her height,
Sank to realms of woe and night,
Wingeth now to heaven her flight.

He whom this world dares not face,
Hath refreshed me with His grace,
And His mighty Hand unbound,
Chains of hell about me wound;
    Quicker, stronger, leaps my blood
    Since His mercy, like a flood,
    Poured o'er all my heart for good.

Bitter anguish have I borne,
Keen regret my heart hath torn,
Sorrow dimmed my weeping eyes,
Satan blinded me with lies:
    Yet at last am I set free,
    Help, protection, love, to me
    Once more true companions be.

Ne'er was left a helpless prey,
Ne'er with shame was turned away,—
He who gave himself to God,
And on him had cast a load;
    Who in God his hope hath placed,
    Shall not life in pain outwaste,
    Fullest joy he yet shall taste.

"REST REMAINETH."

REST REMAINETH—oh, how sweet
Flowery fields for wandering feet,
Peaceful calm for sleepless eyes,
Life for death, and songs for sighs.

Rest remaineth—hush that sigh;
Mourning pilgrim, rest is nigh;
Yet a season, bright and blest,
Thou shalt enter on thy rest.

Rest remaineth—rest from sin—
Guilt can never enter in;
Every warring thought shall cease—
Rest in purity and peace.

Rest remaineth—rest from tears,
Rest from parting, rest from fears;
Every trembling thought shall be
Lost, my Saviour—lost in Thee.

Rest remaineth—oh, how blest!
We believe, and we have rest;
Faith, reposing faith, hath been
'Mongst the things that are not seen.

Thus, my Saviour, let me be
Even here at rest in Thee,
And, at last, by Thee possessed,
On Thy bosom sink to rest.

"I SHALL BE SATISFIED."

NOT HERE! not here! not where the sparkling waters
Fade into mocking sands, as we draw near;
Where in the wilderness each footstep falters:
I shall be satisfied—but oh, not here!

Not here—where every dream of bliss deceives us,
Where the worn spirit never gains its goal;
Where, haunted ever by the thought that grieves us,
Across us floods of bitter memory roll.

There is a land where every pulse is thrilling
With rapture earth's sojourners may not know;
Where heaven's repose the weary heart is stilling
And peacefully life's time-toss'd currents flow.

Far out of sight, while yet the flesh infolds us,
Lies the fair country where our hearts abide,
And of its bliss is naught more wondrous told us
Than these few words: "I shall be satisfied!"

Satisfied! satisfied! the spirit's yearning
For sweet companionship with kindred minds;
The silent love that here meets no returning,
The inspiration which no language finds.

Shall they be satisfied?—the soul's vague longings
The aching void which nothing earthly fills?
O what desires upon my soul are thronging,
As I look upward to the heavenly hills!

Thither my weak and weary feet are tending—
Saviour and Lord, with Thy frail child abide;
Guide me toward home, where, all my wanderings
ended,
I then shall see *Thee* and "be satisfied!"

JESUS, I AM NEVER WEARY.

JESUS, I am never weary,
When upon this bed of pain;
If Thy presence only cheer me,
All my loss I count but gain:
Ever near me,
Ever near me, Lord, remain!

Dear ones come with fruits and flowers,
Thus to cheer my heart the while,

In these deeply anxious hours;
  Oh! if Jesus only smile!—
    Only Jesus
  Can these troubling fears beguile.

All my sins were laid upon Thee,
  All my griefs were on Thee laid;
For the blood of Thine atonement
  All my utmost debts has paid:
    Dearest Saviour!
  I believe, for Thou hast said.

Dearest Saviour! go not from me,
  Let Thy presence still abide;
Look in tenderest love upon me—
  I am sheltering at Thy side,
    Dearest Saviour!
  Who for suffering sinners died.

Both mine arms are clasped around Thee,
  And my head is on Thy breast;
For my weary soul has found Thee
  Such a *perfect, perfect* rest.
    Dearest Saviour!
  Now I know that I am blest.

WE SHALL SEE HIM AS HE IS.

NOT as He was, a houseless stranger,
  With no home to shield His head;
Not as seen in Bethlehem's manger,
  Where the hornéd oxen fed;—

Not as in the Garden groaning,
  Plunged in deep, mysterious woe,
All the guilt of man bemoaning,
  While the precious blood-sweats flow;—

Not as seen on Calvary's mountain,
  Where He offered up His soul,
Opening wide that sacred Fountain,
  Which alone can make us whole;—

Not as He was, a pale and breathless
  Captive in the shades beneath,—
But as He is, Immortal, Deathless,
  Conqueror o'er the powers of death!

Yes! we shall see Him in our nature
  Seated on His lofty Throne—
Loved, adored by every creature—
  Owned as God, and God alone!

There countless hosts of shining spirits
Strike their harps, and loudly sing
To the praise of Jesus' merits,
To the glory of their King!

When we pass o'er death's dark river,
We shall see Him as He is—
Resting in His love and favor,
Owning all the glory His.

There to cast our crowns before Him—
Oh, what bliss the thought affords!
There forever to adore Him—
King of kings and Lord of lords!

CONTENTMENT

BE thou content; be still before
His face, at whose right hand doth reign
Fullness of joy for evermore,
Without whom all thy toil is vain:
He is thy living spring, thy sun, whose rays
Make glad with life and light thy dreary days.
Be thou content.

In Him is comfort, light, and grace,
And changeless love beyond our thought;
The sorest pang, the worst disgrace,
If He is there, shall harm thee not.

He can lift off thy cross, and loose thy bands,
And calm thy fears · nay, death is in His hands:
Be thou content.

Or art thou friendless and alone,
Hast none in whom thou canst confide?
God careth for thee, lonely one—
Comfort and help He will provide.
He sees thy sorrows, and thy hidden grief,
He knoweth when to send thee quick relief:
Be thou content.

Thy heart's unspoken pain He knows,
Thy secret sighs He hears full well;
What to none else thou dar'st disclose,
To Him thou may'st with boldness tell.
He is not far away, but ever nigh,
And answereth willingly the poor man's cry:
Be thou content.

HAVE FAITH IN GOD.

HAVE faith in God! for He who reigns on high
Hath borne thy grief and hears the suppliant's sigh;
Still to His arms, thine only refuge, fly.
Have faith in God!

Fear not to call on Him, O soul distressed!
Thy sorrow's whisper woos thee to His breast;
He who is oftenest there is oftenest blest.
Have faith in God!

Lean not on Egypt's reeds; slake not thy thirst
At earthly cisterns. Seek the kingdom first.
Though man and Satan fright thee with their worst,
Have faith in God!

Go! tell Him all! The sigh thy bosom heaves
Is heard in heaven. Strength and grace He gives,
Who gave Himself for thee. Our Jesus lives.
Have faith in God!

BREAD UPON THE WATERS.

SAY not, "'Twas all in vain,"
The anguish, and the darkness, and the strife;
Love thrown upon the waters comes again
In quenchless yearnings for a nobler life.
Think! In that midnight, on thy weary sight
The stars shone forth, and 'neath their welcome rays
Thine hopes to Heaven like birds first took their flight,
And "thou shalt find them—after many days."

Say not, " 'Twas all in vain,"
The vigil, and the sickness, and the tears;
For in that Land " where there is no more pain,"
The grain is garnered from those mournful years.
The faded form, once sheltered on thy breast,
In gentle ministry thy care repays;
And smiling on thee from her sinless rest,
Fear not to find her—" after many days."

Say not, " 'Twas all in vain,"
Thy tenderness, thy meekness—oh, not so!
A strength for others' sufferings shalt thou gain,
As healing balms from bruiséd flowerets flow.
Weep not the wealth in fearless faith cast forth
On the dark billows shipwrecked to thy gaze;
The bark was frail, the gem had still its worth,
And " thou shalt find it—after many days."

Say not, " 'Twas all in vain,"
The watching, and the waiting, and the prayer;
In piercéd hands hath it unassuméd lain;
'Twill grow more radiant as it lingereth there.
'Tis space—where once thy quivering form was cast,
Thy heart-wrung sobs no floating breeze betrays,
Yet, 'mid the white-winged choir thy prayer hath passed,
And " thou shalt find it—after many days."

Say not, " 'Twas all in vain,"
The patience, and the pity, and the word
In warning breathed 'mid passion's hurricane,
Unheeded here—but God that whisper heard,
The tender grief, o'er strangers' sorrow shed,
The sacrifice that won no human praise.
In faith upon the waters cast thy Bread,
For " thou shalt find it—after many days."

REST FOR THE WEARY.

NOT long, not long! The spirit-wasting fever
Of this strange life shall quit each throbbing vein;
And this wild pulse flow placidly forever;
And endless peace relieve the burning brain.

Earth's joys are but a dream; its destiny
Is but decay and death. Its fairest form
Sunshine and shadow mixed. Its brightest day
A rainbow braided on the wreaths of storm.

Yet there is blessedness that changeth not;
A rest with God, a life that cannot die;
A better portion, and a brighter lot;
A home with Christ, a heritage on high.

Hope for the hopeless, for the weary rest,
  More gentle than the still repose of even!
Joy for the joyless, bliss for the unblest;
  Homes for the desolate in yonder heaven.

The tempest makes returning calm more dear;
  The darkest midnight makes the brightest star;
Even so to us, when all is ended here,
  Shall be the past, remembered from afar.

Then welcome change and death! since these alone
  Can break life's fetters, and dissolve its spell;
Welcome all present change, which speeds us on
  So swift to that which is unchangeable.

THE OFFERING.

NO more my own, Lord Jesus;
  Bought with Thy precious Blood,
I give Thee but Thine own, Lord,
  That long Thy love withstood.

I give the life Thou gavest,
  My present, future, past;
My joys, my fears, my sorrows,
  My first hope and my last.

I give Thee up my weakness,
That oft distrust hath bred,
That Thy indwelling power
May thus be perfected.

I give the love the sweetest
Thy goodness grants to me;
Take it, and make it meet, Lord,
For offering to Thee.

Smile! and the very shadows
In Thy blest light shall shine;
Take Thou my heart, Lord Jesus,
For Thou hast made it Thine.

Thou know'st my soul's ambition,
For Thou hast changed its aim'
(The world's reproach I fear not,)
To share a Saviour's shame;

Outside the camp to suffer;
Within the Vail to meet,
And hear Thy softest whisper
From out the Mercy-seat.

Thou bear'st me on Thy bosom,
Amidst Thy jewels worn,
Upon Thy hands deep graven,
By arms of love upborne.

Rescued from sin's destruction,
 Ransomed from death and hell;
Complete in Thee, Lord Jesus:
 Thou hast done all things well!

Oh, deathless love that bought me!
 Oh, price beyond my ken!
Oh, Life, that hides my own life
 E'en from my fellow-men!

Now fashion, form, and fill me
 With light and love Divine;
So, ONE with Thee, Lord Jesus,
 I'm Thine—forever Thine!

HOLD ON, HOLD IN, HOLD OUT.

HOLD on, my heart, in thy believing!
 The steadfast only wins the crown.
He who, when stormy waves are heaving,
 Parts with his anchor, shall go down;
But he who Jesus holds through all,
Shall stand, though heaven and earth shall fall.

Hold *in* thy murmurs, heaven arraigning!
 The patient see God's loving face:
Who bear their burdens uncomplaining,
 'Tis they that win the Father's grace;

He wounds himself who bears the rod,
And sets himself to fight with God.

Hold *out!* There comes an end to sorrow;
Hope from the dust shall conquering rise;
The storm foretells a sunnier morrow;
The Cross points on to Paradise.
The Father reigneth; cease all doubt;
Hold on, my heart, hold in, hold out!

GO TELL JESUS.

BURY thy sorrow,
The world has its share:
Bury it deeply,
Hide it with care.

Think of it calmly
When curtained by night,
Tell it to Jesus,
And all will be right.

Tell it to Jesus,
He knoweth thy grief;
Tell it to Jesus,
He'll send thee relief.

Gather the sunlight
  Aglow on thy way;
Gather the moonbeams,
  Each soft silver ray.

Hearts grown aweary
  With heavier woe,
Droop 'mid the darkness—
  Go comfort them, go!

Bury thy sorrow,
  Let others be blest;
Give them the sunshine,
  Tell Jesus the rest.

A PSALM FOR NEW YEAR'S EVE

A FRIEND stands at the door;
  In either tight-closed hand
Hiding rich gifts, three hundred and three-score;
  Waiting to strew them daily o'er the land
Even as seed the sower.
  Each drop he treads it in and passes by:
  It cannot be made fruitful till it die.

Oh, good New Year, we clasp
  This warm shut hand of thine!

Loosing forever, with half-sigh, half-grasp,
That which from ours falls like dead fingers' twine:
Ay, whether fierce its grasp
Has been, or gentle, having been, we know
That it was blessed; let the Old Year go.

Oh, New Year, teach us faith!
The road of life is hard;
When our feet bleed, and scourging winds us scathe,
Point thou to Him whose visage was more marred
Than any man's; who saith
"Make straight paths for your feet—" and to the opprest—
"Come ye to Me, and I will give you rest."

Yet hang some lamp-like hope
Above this unknown way,
Kind year, to give our spirits freer scope,
And our hands strength to work while it is day
But if that way must slope
Tombward, oh, bring before our fading eyes
The lamp of life, the Hope that never dies!

Comfort our souls with love,—
Love of all human kind;

Love special, close—in which like sheltered dove
  Each weary heart its own safe nest may find;
And love that turns above
  Adoringly: contented to resign
  All loves, if need be, for the Love Divine.

Friend, come thou like a friend,
  And whether bright thy face,
Or dim with clouds we cannot comprehend,—
  We'll hold our patient hands, each in his place,
And trust thee to the end;
  Knowing thou leadest onwards to those spheres
  Where there are neither days, nor months, nor
    years.

THE CELESTIAL COUNTRY.

THE world is very evil!
  The times are waxing late:
Be sober, and keep vigil;
  The Judge is at the gate:
The Judge That comes in mercy,
  The Judge that comes with might,
To terminate the evil,
  To diadem the right.
When the just and gentle Monarch
  Shall summon from the tomb,

Let man, the guilty, tremble,
 For Man, the God, shall doom
Arise, arise, good Christian,
 Let right to wrong succeed;
Let penitential sorrow
 To heavenly gladness lead;
To the light that hath no evening,
 That knows nor moon nor sun
The light so new and golden,
 The light that is but one.
And when the Sole-Begotten
 Shall render up once more
The kingdom to the FATHER
 Whose own it was before,—
Then glory yet unheard of
 Shall shed abroad its ray,
Resolving all enigmas,
 An endless Sabbath-day.
Then, then from his oppressors
 The Hebrew shall go free,
And celebrate in triumph
 The year of Jubilee;
And the sunlit Land that recks not
 Of tempest nor of fight,
Shall fold within its bosom
 Each happy Israelite:
The Home of fadeless splendor,
 Of flowers that fear no thorn,

Where they shall dwell as children,
  Who here as exiles mourn.
Midst power that knows no limit,
  And wisdom free from bound,
The Beatific Vision
  Shall glad the Saints around:
The peace of all the faithful,
  The calm of all the blest,
Inviolate, unvaried,
  Divinest, sweetest, best.
Yes, peace! for war is needless,—
  Yes, calm! for storm is past,—
And goal from finished labor,
  And anchorage at last.
That peace—but who may claim it?
  The guileless in their way,
Who keep the ranks of battle,
  Who mean the thing they say:
The peace that is for heaven,
  And shall be for the earth:
The palace that re-echoes
  With festal song and mirth;
The garden, breathing spices,
  The paradise on high:
Grace beautified to glory,
  Unceasing minstrelsy.
There nothing can be feeble,
  There none can ever mourn,

There nothing is divided,
  There nothing can be torn:
'Tis fury, ill, and scandal,
  'Tis peaceless peace below;
Peace, endless, strifeless, ageless,
  The halls of Syon know:
O happy, holy portion,
  Refection for the blest·
True vision of true beauty,
  Sweet cure of all distress!
Strive, man, to win that glory;
  Toil, man, to gain that light;
Send hope before to grasp it,
  Till hope be lost in sight:
Till Jesus gives the portion
  Those blessèd souls to fill,
The insatiate, yet satisfied,
  The full, yet craving still.
That fullness and that craving
  Alike are free from pain,
Where thou midst heavenly citizens,
  A home like theirs shalt gain.
Here is the warlike trumpet;
  There, life set free from sin;
When to the last Great Supper
  The faithful shall come in:
When the heavenly net is laden
  With fishes many and great;

So glorious in its fullness,
  Yet so inviolate:
And the perfect from the shattered,
  And the fall'n from them that stand,
And the sheep-flock from the goat-herd
  Shall part on either hand:
And these shall pass to torment,
  And those shall triumph, then;
The new peculiar nation,
  Blest number of blest men.
Jerusalem demands them:
  They paid the price on earth
And now shall reap the harvest
  In blissfulness and mirth:
The glorious holy people,
  Who evermore relied
Upon their Chief and Father,
  The King, the Crucified:
The sacred ransomed number
  Now bright with endless sheen,
Who made the Cross their watch-word
  Of JESUS Nazarene:
Who, fed with heavenly nectar,
  Where foul-like odors play,
Draw out the endless leisure
  Of that long vernal day:
And through the sacred lilies,
  And flowers on every side,

The happy dear-bought people
  Go wandering far and wide.
Their breasts are filled with gladness,
  Their mouths are tuned to praise,
What time, now safe forever,
  On former sins they gaze:
The fouler was the error,
  The sadder was the fall,
The ampler are the praises
  Of Him Who pardoned all.
Their one and only anthem,
  The fullness of His love,
Who gives, instead of torment,
  Eternal joys above:
Instead of torment, glory;
  Instead of death, that life
Wherewith your happy Country,
  True Israelties! is rife.

Brief life is here our portion;
  Brief sorrow, short-lived care
The life that knows no ending
  The tearless life, is *there.*
O happy retribution!
  Short toil, eternal rest;
For mortals and for sinners
  A mansion with the blest!
That we should look, poor wand'rers,

To have our home on high!
That worms should seek for dwellings
Beyond the starry sky!
To all one happy guerdon
Of one celestial grace;
For all, for all, who mourn their fall,
Is one eternal place:
And martyrdom hath roses
Upon that heavenly ground:
And white and virgin lilies
For virgin-souls abound.
There grief is turned to pleasure
Such pleasure, as below
No human voice can utter,
No human heart can know:
And after fleshly scandal,
And after this world's night,
And after storm and whirlwind,
Is calm, and joy, and light.
And now we fight the battle,
But then shall wear the crown
Of full and everlasting
And passionless renown:
And now we watch and struggle
And now we live in hope,
And Syon, in her anguish,
With Babylon must cope:
But He Whom now we trust in

Shall then be seen and known,
And they that know and see Him
Shall have Him for their own.
The miserable pleasures
Of the body shall decay:
The bland and flattering struggles
Of the flesh shall pass away:
And none shall there be jealous;
And none shall there contend:
Fraud, clamor, guile—what say I?
All ill, all ill shall end!
And there is David's Fountain,
And life in fullest glow,
And there the light is golden,
And milk and honey flow:
The light that hath no evening,
The health that hath no sore,
The life that hath no ending,
But lasteth evermore.

There JESUS shall embrace us,
There JESUS be embraced,—
That spirit's food and sunshine
Whence earthly love is chased.
Amidst the happy chorus,
A place, however low,
Shall show Him us, and, showing,
Shall satiate evermo.

By hope we struggle onward.
While here we must be fed
By milk, as tender infants,
But there by Living Bread.
The night was full of terror,
The morn is bright with gladness
The Cross becomes our harbor,
And we triumph after sadness:
And JESUS to His true ones
Brings trophies fair to see:
And JESUS shall be loved, and
Beheld in Galilee:
Beheld, when morn shall waken,
And shadows shall decay,
And each true-hearted servant
Shall shine as doth the day.
And every ear shall hear it:--
Behold thy King's array·
Behold thy GOD in beauty,
The Law hath past away!
Yes! GOD my King and Portion,
In fullness of His grace,
We then shall see forever,
And worship face to face.
Then Jacob into Israel,
From earthlier self estranged,
And Leah into Rachel
Forever shall be changed:

Then all the halls of Syon
  For aye shall be complete,
And, in the Land of Beauty
  All things of beauty meet.

For thee, O dear, dear Country!
  Mine eyes their vigils keep;
For very love, beholding
  Thy happy name, they weep:
The mention of thy glory
  Is unction to the breast,
And medicine in sickness,
  And love, and life, and rest.
O one, O onely Mansion!
  O Paradise of Joy!
Where tears are ever banished,
  And smiles have no alloy;
Beside thy living waters
  All plants are, great and small,
The cedar of the forest,
  The hyssop of the wall:
With jaspers glow thy bulwarks,
  Thy streets with emeralds blaze·
The sardius and the topaz
  Unite in thee their rays:
Thine ageless walls are bonded
  With amethyst unpriced:

Thy Saints build up its fabric,
  And the corner-stone is CHRIST.
The Cross is all thy splendor,
  The Crucified thy praise:
His laud and benediction
  Thy ransomed people raise:
JESUS, the Gem of Beauty,
  True GOD and Man, they sing
The never-failing Garden,
  The ever-golden Ring:
The Door, the Pledge, the Husband,
  The Guardian of his Court:
The Day-star of Salvation,
  The Porter and the Port.
Thou hast no shore, fair ocean!
  Thou hast no time, bright day!
Dear fountain of refreshment
  To pilgrims far away!
Upon the Rock of Ages
  They raise thy holy tower:
Thine is the victor's laurel,
  And thine the golden dower:
Thou feel'st in mystic rapture,
  O Bride that know'st no guile,
The Prince's sweetest kisses,
  The Prince's loveliest smile;
Unfading lilies, bracelets
  Of living pearl thine own;

The LAMB is ever near thee,
  The Bridegroom thine alone;
The Crown is He to guerdon,
  The Buckler to protect,
And He Himself the Mansion
  And He the Architect.
The only art thou needest,
  Thanksgiving for thy lot:
The only joy thou seekest,
  The Life where Death is not
And all thine endless leisure
  In sweetest accents sings,
The ill that was thy merit,—
  The wealth that is thy King's

Jerusalem the golden,
  With milk and honey blest,
Beneath thy contemplation
  Sink heart and voice oppressed:
I know not, O I know not,
  What social joys are there;
What radiancy of glory,
  What light beyond compare!
And when I fain would sing them,
  My spirit fails and faints;
And vainly would it image
  The assembly of the Saints.
They stand, those halls of Syon,

Conjubilant with song,
And bright with many an angel,
And all the martyr throng:
The Prince is ever in them;
The daylight is serene;
The pastures of the Blessèd
Are decked in glorious sheen.
There is the throne of David,—
And there, from care released,
The song of them that triumph,
The shout of them that feast:
And they who, with their Leader,
Have conquered in the fight,
Forever and forever
Are clad in robes of white!

O holy, placid harp-notes
Of that eternal hymn!
O sacred, sweet refection,
And peace of Seraphim!
O thirst, forever ardent,
Yet evermore content!
O true peculiar vision
Of God cunctipotent!
Ye know the many mansions
For many a glorious name,
And divers retributions
That divers merits claim:

For midst the constellations
  That deck our earthly sky,
This star than that is brighter,—
  And so it is on high.

Jerusalem the glorious!
  The glory of th' Elect!
O dear and future vision
  That eager hearts expect;
Even now by faith I see thee;
  Even here thy walls discern:
To thee my thoughts are kindled.
  And strive and pant and yearn:
Jerusalem the onely,
  That look'st from heaven below.
In thee is all my glory;
  In me is all my woe:
And though my body may not,
  My spirit seeks thee fain,
Till flesh and earth return me
  To earth and flesh again.
O none can tell thy bulwarks,
  How gloriously they rise:
O none can tell thy capitals
  Of beautiful device:
Thy loveliness oppresses
  All human thought and heart:

And none, O peace, O Syon,
  Can sing thee as thou art.
New mansion of new people,
  Whom GOD's own love and light
Promote, increase, make holy,
  Identify, unite.
Thou City of the Angels!
  Thou City of the Lord!
Whose everlasting music
  Is the glorious decachord!*
And there the band of Prophets
  United praise ascribes,
And there the twelve-fold chorus
  Of Israel's ransomed tribes:
The lily-beds of virgins,
  The roses' martyr-glow,
The cohort of the Fathers
  Who kept the faith below.
And there the Sole-Begotten
  Is LORD in regal state;
He, Judah's mystic Lion,
  He, Lamb Immaculate.
O fields that know no sorrow!
  O state that fears no strife!

* *Decachord.* With reference to the mystical explanation which, seeing in the number *ten* a type of perfection, understands the "instrument of ten strings" of the perfect harmony of heaven.

O princely bow'rs! O land of flow'rs!
  O realm and home of life!

Jerusalem, exulting
  On that securest shore,
I hope thee, wish thee, sing thee,
  And love thee evermore!
I ask not for my merit:
  I seek not to deny
My merit is destruction,
  A child of wrath am I:
But yet with Faith I venture
  And Hope upon my way;
For those perennial guerdons
  I labor night and day.
The Best and Dearest FATHER
  Who made me and Who saved,
Bore with me in defilement,
  And from defilement laved:
When in His strength I struggle,
  For very joy I leap,
When in my sin I totter,
  I weep, or try to weep:
And grace, sweet grace celestial,
  Shall all its love display,
And David's Royal Fountain
  Purge every sin away.

O mine, my golden Syon!
  O lovelier far than gold!
With laurel-girt battalions,
  And safe victorious fold:
O sweet and blessèd Country,
  Shall I ever see thy face?
O sweet and blessèd Country,
  Shall I ever win thy grace?
I *have* the hope within me
  To comfort and to bless!
Shall I ever win the prize itself?
  O tell me, tell me, Yes!

Exult, O dust and ashes!
  The LORD shall be thy part:
His only, His forever,
  Thou shalt be, and thou art!
Exult, O dust and ashes!
  The LORD shall be thy part:
His only, His forever,
  Thou shalt be, and thou art!

"TAKE HEART OF GRACE."

OH, thou! who tossing on life's troubled ocean,
  Mournest the hidings of thy Father's face,
And comfortless, amid the wild commotion,
  Seekest in vain some quiet resting-place;
  Thou weary, fainting soul! "take heart of grace."

Look up! when storms of woe are round thee sweeping,
  Learn thou in all thy Saviour's hand to trace:
Above the storm, behind the dark clouds, keeping
  Ceaseless watch o'er thee, beams my loving face;
  Therefore, thou faithless one! take heart of grace.

Not all the fiercest tempests round thee blowing,
  Can drive thee far from heaven's sweet resting-place;
Not all the floods thy sorrowing soul o'erflowing,
  Can long avail to hide from thee my face;
  Therefore, O downcast soul! take heart of grace.

Oh, waste no more thy breath in weak complaining!
  Doubts throw aside! No longer thus disgrace
My faithful love that leading, guiding, training,

Perfects thee thus for my own dwelling-place.
O thou rebellious soul! take heart of grace.

Hast thou not seen how, for some precious treasure,
Men beat of purest gold, a goodly case?
Or cut for fragrant odors, at their pleasure,
Out of rough stone, a rare and polished vase?
O thou short-sighted one! take heart of grace.

Like them, when for myself I am preparing
Out of the soul, a fit abiding-place;
I hew thee, beat thee, till I see thee bearing
My image; and my perfect likeness trace;
Therefore, thou chosen one! take heart of grace.

Oh then, be of good courage! for I love thee,
Gladly and cheerfully each cross embrace,
And bear it manfully; for soon above thee,
Light from my throne each cloud away shall chase;
Therefore, afflicted one! take heart of grace.

And soon life's sorest trials passed forever,
Faultless before thy and my Father's face,
I will present thee joyfully; and never
Need to say to thee, in that resting-place,
O weary, fainting soul! take heart of grace.

For every hour of that blest life immortal,
Thou shalt be glad my guiding hand to trace,
That made thee meet, by trials, through the portal
To enter in, and rest in my embrace;
Therefore, look upward! and take heart of grace.

BECAUSE HE FIRST LOVED US

I LOVE Thee, O my God! but not
For what I hope thereby,
Nor yet because who love Thee not
Must die eternally.
I love Thee, O my God! and still
I ever will love Thee,
Solely because, my God, Thou art
Who first hast lovéd me!

For me, to lowest depths of woe
Thou didst Thyself abase;
For me didst bear the cross, the shame,
And manifold disgrace;
For me didst suffer pains unknown,
Blood-sweat and agony.
Yea, death itself—all, all for me!
For me, Thine enemy!

Then shall I not, O Saviour, mine!
  Shall I not love Thee well?
Not with the hope of winning heaven,
  Nor of escaping hell;
Not with the hope of earning aught,
  Nor seeking a reward;
But freely, fully, as Thyself
  Hast lovéd me, O Lord!

SICK AND IN PRISON.

WILDLY falls the night around me,
  Chains I cannot break have bound me
Spirits unrebuked, undriven
From before me darken Heaven;
Creeds bewilder, and the saying
Unfelt prayer makes need of praying.

In this bitter anguish lying
Only Thou wilt hear my crying—
Thou whose hands wash white the erring,
As the wool is at the shearing,
Not with dulcimer or psalter,
But with tears, I seek Thine altar.

Feet, that trod the mount so weary,
Eyes, that pitying looked on Mary,
Hands, that brought a Father's blessing,
Heads of little children pressing;
Voice, that said, "Behold thy Mother,"
Lo! I seek ye, and none other.

Look, O gentlest eye of pity,
Out of Zion, glorious city!
Speak, O voice of mercy, sweetly!
Hide me, hands of love, completely.
Sick, in prison, lying lonely,
Ye can lift me up—Ye only.

In my hot brow soothe the aching,
In my sad heart stay the breaking;
On my lips, the murmurs trembling
Change to praises undissembling;
Make me raise as th' evangels,
Clothe me with the wings of angels.

Power, that made the few loaves many,
Power, that blessed the wine at Cana,
Power, that said to Lazarus "waken,"
Leave, oh, leave me not forsaken,
Sick, and hungry, and in prison,
Save me, Crucified and Risen!

"AS ONE WHOM HIS MOTHER COMFORTETH."

"SO will I comfort you," as when a sobbing child
Seeks sweet heart-comfort on its mother's breast;
By her caresses fond unconsciously beguiled
From memories of pain, soon sinks to rest.

"Ye shall be comforted." Our hearts are faint and sore.
We would be little children once again;
But childhood would bring back the griefs we knew of yore,
But not the mother who caressed us then.

We need a stronger love, we seek a deeper rest,
Whose type and earnest we once knew in this;
The nestling of the child upon its mother's breast,
The sweet dreams won us by her "good-night" kiss.

Lord! grant us restful sleep, untroubled, sweet and calm,
Not fitful slumbers 'mid Life's fevered dream;
Oh, seal our weary eyelids with thy touch of balm
Not to re-ope until the Great Day's gleam.

And yet we are such children, foolish, weak and blind,
That while we long for sleep, thy gentle hand
May change the calming cup, and far more wise and kind,
Give needed bitterness with this command:

"Drink, child!" Thy Father's love shall make the unsought draught
Sweet to thy soul, though bitter to thy lips.
Think, how for thee, thy sinless Elder Brother quaffed
The cup thou filled'st, 'neath my love's eclipse.

Ah, Father! whatsoe'er thy children truly need
Thou givest, not whatever they implore.
And oft we grieving think, Thy mercy gives no heed
To our rash pleadings, when our hearts are sore.

But when the long sad lesson we have learned a length,
And with unmurmuring meekness we receive
The cup, whose bitter draught gives new and mighty strength,
We own Thy wise true love, and no more grieve

But rest in patient hope, although Thou long withhold
The chalice. Death and Life brimmed, chrismal seal
Of conquest at whose touch the pearly gates unfold,
And Heaven's high glories to the soul reveal.

We only wait as minors, till the glad birth-day
Shall crown us kings before our Father's throne.
As princely exiles here, we struggle, toil, and pray,
With eyes by watching very weary grown.

For comfortless, aye, orphan'd, Thou dost never make
Thy children. Trusting hearts are kept in peace,
And when our night-time comes, Thou'lt bid us sleep to wake
Where every sob is hushed and sorrows cease.

MARY.

THE box is not of stainless alabaster
Which o'er thy feet I break;
Nor filled with costly ointment, gracious Master,
Poured for Thy sake.

Nay, rather is it shapen in this fashion—
A living heart,
Dashed all across with scarlet stains of passion,
And broke in part;

While from its open wound comes softly dripping
Like slow tears shed,
Or heavy drops, along thy footstool slipping,
Its life-blood red.

It needs no balm of myrrh for sweet or bitter,
But life and love;
The sad conditions make mine offering fitter
Thy heart to move.

From all these claims of cruel wrong and anguish,
This load of grief
Wherewith my soul doth pant, and mourn, and lan-

In thy far home is not thy soul still tender
  For mortal woe?
Hear'st thou not still, amid that spotless splendor
  That seraphs know?

O, turn thy human eyes from heavenly glory!
  Say, as before,
Those tenderest words of all thy Gospel story:
  "Go, sin no more!"

EVENING.

GENTLY the dew falls on the grass,
  The winds are hushed to rest,
And softly sinks the crescent moon,
  Adown the quiet west.

And one by one, as shadows fall,
  The stars come out on high,
Till in full brightness spreads unveiled,
  The glory of the sky,

I sit upon the summer hills,
  Far from the noisy throng,
And hear the modest night-bird sing
  Her low and plaintive song.

The little streamlets bright and clear
  Go singing on their way,

While countless insect voices weave
  Their never-ending lay.

O God, in such an hour as this,
  How yearns the soul to know
The mysteries of the heavens above
  And of the earth below!

An atom in the boundless whole,
  A speck upon the air,
I seem as one engulfed and lost,
  Without a Father's care.

My life I draw, I know not how.
  From the mysterious past;
Before me stretches all unknown
  A future strange and vast.

What part have I in this wide realm?
  What place have I to fill?
Or can the smallest issue hang
  Upon my wavering will?

Yet folded in these shades of night,
  My busy thoughts arise,
To range afar the fields of earth,
  And wander through the skies.

Is there a hand that reaches down
  From out this vast unknown?
Is there a love that beckons me
  To the eternal throne?

I ask the silent stars above,
  As men have asked of old,
No voice comes from them, as they look,
  On mountains still and cold.

The entrance of Thy Word, O God!
  Alone can break this night,
And shed o'er all the way I go,
  A clear and living light.

By faith, I take that blessed Word
  And follow at its call;
The God who made the heavens and earth,
  Can see and know them all.

HIS WAYS.

I ASKED for grace to lift me high,
  Above the world's depressing cares,
God sent me sorrows—with a sigh
  I said, He has not heard my prayers.

I asked for light, that I might see
  My path along life's thorny road;
But clouds and darkness shadowed me
  When I expected light from God.

I asked for peace, that I might rest
  To think my sacred duties o'er,
When lo! such horrors filled my breast
  As I had never felt before.

And O I cried, can this be prayer
  Whose plaints the steadfast mountains move?
Can this be Heaven's prevailing care;
  And, O my God, is this Thy love?

But soon I found that sorrow, worn
  As Duty's garment, strength supplies,
And out of darkness meekly borne
  Unto the righteous light doth rise.

And soon I found that fears which stirr'd
  My startled soul God's will to do,
On me more real peace conferr'd
  Than in life's calm I ever knew.

Then, Lord, in Thy mysterious ways
  Lead my dependent spirit on,
And whensoe'er it kneels and prays,
  Teach it to say, "Thy will be done!"

Let its one thought, one hope, one prayer,
  Thine image seek—Thy glory see;
Let every other wish and care
  Be left confidingly to Thee!

STRENGTH FOR THE DAY.

STRENGTH for the day! At early dawn I stand,
  Helpless and weak, and with unrested eyes,
  Watching for day. Before its portal lies
A low black cloud—a heavy iron band:
Slowly the mist is lifted from the land,
  And pearl and amber gleam across the skies,
  Gladdening my upward gaze with sweet surprise!
I own the sign: I know that He whose hand
  Hath fringed those sombre clouds with ruby ray,
And changed that iron bar to molten gold,
  Will to my wandering steps be guide and stay—
  Breathe o'er my wavering heart His rest for aye,
And give my waiting, folded palms to hold
  His blessed morning boon—strength for the day

IN THE HARVEST FIELD.

GLORY to Him who bids the field
  Its blessing to our toil to yield,
Who giveth much, who giveth more,

Till store and basket runneth o'er;
Thus, ere the golden skies grow dim,
Come, let us sing our Harvest hymn.

His finger on the land doth lay
Its beauty, stretching far away;
His breath doth fill the opal skies
With grandeur dread to mortal eyes;
He gives man harvest from the wild,
And drops the daisies for the child.

But oh, how shall we dare draw near?
Such power is veiled in mists of fear,
What can we be to One who fills
The awful silence of the hills,
Who knows the secrets of the sea,
The wild beasts in the forests free?

But, Lord, we know Thee otherwise—
A slighted man, with loving eyes,
Toiling along with weary feet
Such paths as these among the wheat;
Come from the light of Heaven's throne
To call no home on earth Thine own.

O Lord, Thou givest bounteous spoil
To the poor measure of our toil,
For our few gray dark sowing days
The glow of August's evening blaze.

And what can we give for the pain
With which Thou sowed immortal grain?

Nothing—for all we have is Thine,
Who need'st not corn, nor oil, nor wine;
Nothing—unless Thou make us meet
To follow Thee through tares and wheat,
And from the storm of wrath and sin
To help Thee bring Thy harvest in.

NOT AS THE WORLD GIVETH.

CLEARER than vision of inspired dreamer!
Dearer than hope of glories yet to be!
Fall on the heart, Thy words, O blest Redeemer—
"Not as the world giveth give I unto thee!"

Not as the world giveth, though her fields are waving
White with her incense-flowers, like foam upon the sea;
Not though her singing birds their earth-born songs are saving
'Till in the upper air they pour them out to Thee;

Not though the fair of earth still with sweet endeavor,
Set firm white faces 'gainst the tide of wrong;

Not though love's monotone and children's voices
ever
Hide in the harmonies of earth's purest song;

Not though Faith, victorious, seizes Earth's high
places,
Sets over all the steady star of Hope;
Not though Love that suffereth and is kind, her traces
Leaves on the soul, that scarce with flesh can cope;

Not with earthly splendor, though her days in dying
Lie down in blue and gold, and wrap themselves in
flame;
Not though the saints of God in her still valleys
lying,
Write o'er their resting-places, "Hallowed be Thy
name;"

Not as the world giveth, though her trees and
grasses
Climb her high mountains and cluster in her clouds;
Not as the world giveth, though her fame, that
passes,
Gilds with brief glory her kings in purple shrouds;

Not as the world giveth, though her hand be laden
Heavy with the jewels earth still holds for man;
Not as the world giveth, though a man and maiden
Know, for a moment, more than angel can.

Not such as these, that leave no sign in dying,
Is the dear Voice—we know it to be true—
That through the ages to the saints is crying,
"Not as the world giveth give I unto you."

A SAVIOUR'S LOVE.

"LOVE I Thee, Lord? How much love I?
Truly, Lord, I cannot tell."
"Yet thou lov'st Me?" "Yes, I love Thee,
Love Thee passing, passing well.

"I would give all hoped-for glory
Gladly yield my slender all,
To behold Thy face forever,
At Thy blessed feet to fall.

"Yes, I love Thee as I never
Loved upon this earth before;
I have loved, intensely, wildly,
Yet, oh, Lord! I love Thee more."

"Try, my child, *My* love to measure."
"Rising heights each height transcend."
"Sink the plummet!" "Lord, 'tis weary,
And it cannot find the end."

RABBONI.

I.

Of all the nights of most mysterious dread,
 This elded earth hath known, none matched
 in gloom
That crucifixion night when Christ lay dead,
 —Sealed up in Joseph's tomb!

II.

No faith that rose sublime above the pain,
 Remembered in its anguish what He said;
"After three days and I shall rise again,"
 —Their hopeless hearts were dead.

III.

Throughout the ghastly "Preparation Day,"
 How had that stricken mother dragged her breath
 Like all of Adam born, her God-given lay
 Beneath the doom of death.

IV.

The prophecy she nursed through pondering years
 Of apprehension, now had found its whole
Fulfillment, infinite beyond her fears,
 —The sword *had* pierced her soul!

V.

The vehement tears of Peter well might flow,
Mixed with the wormwood of repentant shame;
Now would he yield his life thrice told, if so
He might confess the name

VI.

He had denied with curses. Fruitless were
The keen remorses now, the gnawing smart;
A heavier stone than sealed the sepulchre
Was rolled above his heart.

VII.

Surprise and grief and baffled hopes sufficed
To rush as seas their souls and God between;
Yet none of all had mourned the buried Christ,
As Mary Magdalene.

VIII.

When all condemned—He bade her live again,
When all were hard—His pity moved above
Her penitent spirit, healed it, cleansed its stain,
And made it pure with love.

IX.

And she had broken all her costliest store
O'er him whose tenderness, so new, so rare,
Stood like a strong, white angel evermore
'Twixt her and mad despair.

X.

And He was dead!—Her peace had died with him!
The demons who had fled at his control,
With sevenfold chains within their dungeons dim,
Would henceforth bind her soul.

XI.

How slowly crept the Sabbath's endless week!
What aching vigils watched the lingering day,
When she might stagger through the dark and seek
The garden where He lay!

XII.

And when she thrid her way to meet the dawn,
And found the gates unbarred,—a grieving moan
Broke from her lips—"Who," for her strength was
"Will roll away the stone?" [gone—

XIII.

She held no other thought, no hope but this;
To look—to touch the sacred flesh once more,—
Handle the spices with adoring kiss,
And help to wind him o'er

XIV.

With the fair linen Joseph had prepared,—
Lift reverently the wounded hands and feet,
And gaze, one blinded, on the features bared,
And drink the last, most sweet,

XV.

Divine illusion of his presence there;
  And then, the embalming done, with one low cry
Of utmost, unappeasable despair,
  Seek out her home and die.

XVI.

Lo! the black square that showed the opened tomb!
  She sprang—she entered unafraid—and swept
Her arms outstretching, groping through the gloom,
  To touch Him where He slept.

XVII.

Her trembling fingers grasped the raiment cold,
  Pungent with aloes, lying where He lay:
She smoothed her hands above it, fold by fold,—
  Her Lord was stolen away!—

XVIII.

And others came anon, who wept him sore,—
  Simon and John, the women pale and spent
With fearful watchings; wondering more and more
  They questioned, gazed,—and went.

XIX.

Nor thus did Mary. Though the lingering gloom
  Parted into brightness, and city's stir
Came floating upward to the golden tomb,
  There was no dawn for her:

XX.

No room for faintest hopes, nor utmost fears;
For when she sobbing stooped, and saw the twain
White-clothen angels, through her falling tears,
Sit where her Lord had lain,—

XXI.

And ask,—"Why weepest thou?"—there brake no cry,
But she with deaden'd calm her answer made:
"Because they have taken away my Lord, and I
Know not where He is laid."

XXII.

—Was it a step upon the dewy grass?
Was it a garment rustled by the wind?
Did some hushed breathing o'er her senses pass,
And draw her looks behind?

XXIII.

She turned and saw—the very Lord she sought—
Jesus, the newly-risen! . . . but no surprise
Held her astound and rooted to the spot;
Her film'd and holden eyes

XXIV.

Had only vision for the swathèd form;
Nor from her mantle lifted she her face,
Nor marveled that the gardener's voice should warm
With pity at her case;—

XXV.

Till sprang the sudden thought, "If *he* should
know:"—
And then she turned full quickly: "Sir, I pray
Tell me where thou hast borne Him, that I may go
And take Him thence away."

XXVI.

The resurrection-morning's broadening blaze
Shot up behind, and clear before her sight,
Centered on Jesus its transfiguring rays,
And hallowed Him with light.

XXVII.

"*Mary!*"—The measureless pathos was the same
As when her Lord had said—"Thou art forgiven:"
Had he, for comfort, named her by her name
Out from the height of heaven?

XXVIII.

She looked aloft—she listened, turned and gazed;
A revelation flashed across her brow;
One moment,—and she prostrate fell, amazed,—
"*Rabboni!—It is Thou!*"

TO THEE!

I BRING my sins to Thee,
  The sins I cannot count,
That all may cleansed be
  In Thy once-opened fount.
I bring them, Saviour, all to Thee;
  The burden is too great for me.

My heart to Thee I bring,
  The heart I cannot read;
A faithless, wandering thing,
  An evil heart indeed.
I bring it, Saviour, now to Thee,
That fixed and faithful it may be.

To Thee I bring my care,
  The care I cannot flee;
Thou wilt not only share,
  But take it all for me.
O loving Saviour! now to Thee,
I bring the load that wearies me.

I bring my grief to Thee,
  The grief I cannot tell;
No words shall needed be,
  Thou knowest all so well.
I bring the sorrow laid on me,
O suffering Saviour! all to Thee.

My joys to Thee I bring,
  The joys Thy love has given,
That each may be a wing
  To lift me nearer heaven.
I bring them, Saviour, all to Thee,
Who hast procured them all for me.

My life I bring to Thee,
  I would not be my own;
O Saviour! let me be
  Thine ever, Thine alone!
My heart, my life, my all I bring
To Thee, my Saviour and my King.

INDWELLING.

IN unto me, Oh Christ, Divine One, come!
  I'll open wide the door. Make me Thy Temple, home.
Cleanse Thou each hidden chamber of my soul;
Cure secret sickness,—make me perfect,—whole.
Cast out—to stay cast out—all love of sin.
Adorn, with Thine own hand, the dwelling-place within.
Let me Thy presence feel. Mine eyes Thy glory see.
My guest, abiding guest, oh! wilt Thou be?
Spread Thou the table; let me sup with Thee—
Come unto me!

Long years I've wandered in this world of woe,
In by-paths strange and devious would I go;
With books of learning, I have vainly sought
To feed my soul—to wholly live on thought,
Till now half starved, emaciate, poor and lean,
I find myself all naked, sick, unclean—
Unfit at any table to appear,
Convulsed by doubts and sore distressed by fear;
Yet still I need Thee, Lord, and fain would be
Thy host and guest, from all uncleanness free:
Come unto me!
Oh, come to me!

My heart I'll open wide. There's not a room,
So high or low, but to it Thou shalt come,
From attic high to cellar dark and drear,
Where oft I've sought for peace or fled in fear;
Where e'en my dearest friend has ne'er been bid;
Where all my secret motives have been hid—
All, *all*—I open wide—the house is Thine
Within to dwell, to feast, and evermore to shine.
Let me belong to Thee! and be Thou mine,
My only Guest—my Deity!—
Come unto me!
Oh, come to me.

Henceforth I feast; but at no cost of mine;
Henceforth I drink life-giving, heavenly wine;
Henceforth, with flowers are crowned my every cup.
Henceforth with Jesus as my guest I sup.

Henceforth my mind, my heart, my being whole
Is made a glorious palace for the soul;
And at its table, most divinely spread,
I feast, and feast again, on Living Bread;—
Nothing to hide,—there is no future dread;
Here, with my Friend, my Brother, Priest and King,
Joy fills my every sense. His praises now I sing,
And day by day, new beauties do I see,
For He has come to me,
Even unto me.

WAIT ON THE LORD.

ONE touch from Thee—the Healer of diseases;
One little touch would make our brother whole;
And yet Thou comest not—O blessed Jesus!
Send a swift answer to our waiting soul.

Full many a message have we sent, and pleaded
That Thou wouldst haste Thy coming, gracious Lord;
Each message was received, and heard, and heeded,
And yet we welcome no responsive word.

We know that Thou art blessing whilst withholding;
We know that Thou art near us, though apart;
And though we list no answer, Thou art folding
Our poor petitions to thy smitten heart.

A bright and glorious answer is preparing,
Hid in the heights of love—the depths of grace;
We know that Thou, the Risen, still art bearing
Our cause as Thine within the holy place

And so we trust our pleadings to Thy keeping;
So at Thy feet we lay our burden down;
Content to bear the earthly cross, with weeping,
Till at Thy feet we cast the heavenly crown.

MY PRAYER.

GIVE me a song, and I will sing it!
Give me an offering, I will bring it!
Give me Thyself, and I will take Thee!
Withdraw Thyself, and I forsake Thee!
My land lies fallow: Master, till me!
My heart lies empty: Master, fill me!
It plays the traitor: Master, win me!
It faints! it dies! Put new life in me!
It goes astray: good Shepherd, lead me!
It sighs for hunger: come and feed me!
It is so poor! Give riches to me!
It is corrupt: O Lord, renew me!
So ignorant! Oh! wilt Thou teach me?
Has wandered far! But Thou canst reach me!
Is sore diseased: Physician, heal me!
Exposed to danger: oh, conceal me!
It trembles! In Thine arms, oh, fold me!
Begins to sink! O Saviour, hold me!
Is sinking fast! Lord, look upon me!
So cold and dark! Oh, shine upon me!
A poor, lost sinner! Come and find me!

A rebel! May Thy love now bind me!
A prodigal! Wilt Thou receive me?
A beggar! Oh! wilt Thou relieve me?
A backslider! Wilt Thou restore me?
Unholy! May Thy presence awe me!
Unfit to die! O God, prepare me!
So weak! On eagles' wings, oh, bear me!
So comfortless! Lord Jesus, cheer me!
So lonely! God of love, draw near me!
By sin accused! Good Lord, acquit me!
Unfit for Heaven's pure service! Fit me!
Unfit for work on earth! But use me!
A suppliant! Do not Thou refuse me!
Oh! come and fill the hungry with good things:
For Thou hast all I need, Thou King of kings!

LIGHT OF THE WORLD.

LIGHT of the World! to Thee I come!
All dark with sin am I;
Yet is thy light my childhood's home,
Long lost: now through the earth I roam
A stranger, wearily.

Though I am dark, Thou seest me,
And knowest all my sin;
I cannot hide one thought from Thee—
Nor would I, Lord! O search, and see
All that lies hid within!

Unless I know my Father knows
The worst that I have done,
How can I bear the love He shows?
How take the gift that love bestows
On such a guilty one?

My Father, lo, all doubting dies!
I *know* that Thou canst see.
Outspread before Thy glorious eyes
My present, past, and future lies;
And yet Thou lovest me!

NOT LOST.

THE look of sympathy, the gentle word,
Spoken so low that only angels heard;
The secret art of pure self-sacrifice,
Unseen by men but marked by angels' eyes;
These are not lost.

The sacred music of a tender strain,
Wrung from a poet's heart by grief and pain,
And chanted timidly, with doubt and fear,
To busy crowds who scarcely pause to hear,
It is not lost.

The prayers that rise like incense from the soul,
Longing for Christ to make it clean and whole;
These are not lost.

The happy dreams that gladdened all our youth,
When dreams had less of self and more of truth
The childlike faith, so tranquil and so sweet,
Which sat like Mary at the Master's feet;
These are not lost.

The kindly plans devised for others' good,
So seldom guessed, so little understood;
The quiet, steadfast love that strove to win
Some wanderer from the woeful ways of sin;
These are not lost.

Not lost, O Lord, for in Thy city bright,
Our eyes shall see the past by clearer light;
And things long hidden from our gaze below,
Thou wilt reveal, and we shall surely know
They were not lost.

JERUSALEM ABOVE IS FREE.

I WOULD not stay the years that wing,
Howe'er my lot be cast,
Nor say, O sun, look back, and bring
One day from out the past.

He ever will my portion be
  Whose goodness I recall—
Jerusalem above is free,
  And mother of us all.

Free are her happy gates to prayer,
  And open night and day,
The holy lyres are tuneful there
  When earthworn pilgrims pray;
There wakes the strain of jubilee
  When helpless sinners call—
Jerusalem above is free,
  And mother of us all.

Free are the fadeless bowers of rest,
  And free their joys untold,
Free are the mansions of the blest,
  And free the streets of gold.
Though hidden long the glories be
  Salvation is the wall—
Jerusalem above is free,
  And mother of us all.

Home of my soul! I praise the Lord
  That made thy comforts free,
And led me by His faithful word
  To seek my rest in Thee!
Though circumscribed my way may be,
  I know, whate'er befall,
Jerusalem above is free,
  And mother of us all

I would not stay the years that wing,
  Howe'er my lot be cast,
Nor say, O sun, look back, and bring
  One day from out the past.
He ever will my portion be
  Whose goodness I recall—
Jerusalem above is free,
  And mother of us all.

LIVING WATERS.

THERE are some hearts like wells, green-mossed and deep
    As ever summer saw;
And cool their water is—yea, cool and sweet;—
    But you must come to draw.
They hoard not, yet they rest in calm content,
    And not unsought will give;
They can be quiet with their wealth unspent,
    So self-contained they live.

And there are some like springs, that bubbling burst
    To follow dusty ways,
And run with offered cup to quench his thirst
    Where the tired traveler strays:—
That never ask the meadows if they want
    What is their joy to give—
Unasked, their lives to other life they grant—
    So self-bestowed they live!

And One is like the ocean, deep and wide,
Wherein all waters fall;
That girdles the broad earth, and draws the tide,
Feeding and bearing all.
That broods the mists, that sends the clouds abroad
That takes, again to give;
Even the great and loving heart of God,
Whereby all love doth live.

AT EVENING.

UNDER Thy loving care
Another day has past;
Its sacrifice I bear
To Thee at last.

Thou knowest every cross,
Each pleasure and each pain;
Thou seest what is loss,
And what is gain.

These tangled threads of life
Thou holdest in thy hand,
And thou their seeming strife
Dost understand.

So in thy loving care
I rest secure, forgiven;
Thou wilt the morrow's work prepare,
Or give me Heaven.

MY CROSS.

IT is not heavy agonizing woe,
Bearing me down with hopeless, crushing weight
No ray of comfort in the gathering gloom;
A heart bereaved, a household desolate.

It is not sickness with her withering hand,
Keeping me low upon a couch of pain;
Longing each morning for the weary night,
At night for weary day to come again.

It is not poverty with chilling blast,
The sunken eye, the hunger-wasted form;
The dear ones perishing for lack of bread,
With no safe shelter from the winter's storm.

It is not slander with her evil tongue;
'Tis not "presumptuous sins" against my God;
Not reputation lost, nor friends betrayed;
That such is not my cross, I thank my God.

Mine is a daily cross of petty cares,
Of little duties pressing on my heart,
Of little troubles hard to reconcile,
Of inward troubles overcome in part.

My feet are weary in their daily rounds,
My heart is weary of its daily care,

My sinful nature often doth rebel:
I pray for grace my daily cross to bear.

It is not heavy, Lord, yet oft I pine!
It is not heavy, but 'tis everywhere;
By day and night each hour my cross I bear,
I dare not lay it down—Thou keep'st it there.

I dare not lay it down; I only ask
That, taking up my daily cross, I may
Follow my Master, humbly, step by step,
Through clouds and darkness unto perfect day.

ALONE WITH GOD.

ALONE with Thee, my God! alone with Thee!
Thus wouldst Thou have it still—thus let it be
There is a secret chamber in each mind,
Which none can find
But He who made it—none beside can know
Its joy or woe.
Oft may I enter it, oppressed by care,
And find Thee there;
So full of watchful love, Thou know'st the why
Of every sigh.
Then all Thy righteous dealings shall I see,
Alone with Thee, my God! alone with Thee.

The joys of earth are like a summer's day,
Fading away;
But in the twilight we may better trace
Thy wondrous grace.
The homes of earth are emptied oft by death
With chilling breath;
The loved departed guest may ope no more
The well-known door;
Still in that chamber seal'd Thou'lt dwell with me,
And I with Thee, my God! alone with Thee.

The world's false voice would bid me enter not
That hallowed spot;
And earthly thoughts would follow on the track
To hold me back,
Or seek to break the sacred peace within
With this world's din.
But, by Thy grace, I'll cast them all aside,
Whate'er betide;
And never let that cell deserted be,
Where I may dwell alone, my God, with Thee.

The war may rage!—keep Thou the citadel,
And all is well.
And when I learn the fullness of Thy love
With Thee above—
When every heart oppressed by hidden grief
Shall gain relief—

When every weary soul shall find its rest
Amidst the blest—
Then all my heart, from sin and sorrow free,
Shall be a temple meet, my God, for Thee!

THE BATTLE FOUGHT AND WON.

COME, Lord, and fight the battle,
My hands are tired and faint:
I have no strength to struggle,
"Consider my complaint."
One of Thy weakest soldiers
Is weary in the field,—
Yet Thine is all the victory,
Thy love is all my shield.

'Tis not that I am weary
Of service done for Thee;—
'Tis not that I would alter
Thy loving will for me—
Sweet is the vineyard labor,
Through all the toil and heat;
And sweet the lonely night-watch
Safe resting at Thy feet.

Yet, Lord, there is a warfare
No eye but Thine may see;
Oh, hear my cry for succor,
Come Thou, and fight for me.

The self I cannot conquer,
  The will that still is mine,
Oh, take them both, Lord Jesus,
  And make them one with Thine.

Take them! I cannot yield them—
  I am not what I seemed:
I have no power, Lord Jesus,
  To do what once I dream'd.
The yearning of the earth-life,
  Is stronger than my strength;
When may the spell be broken,
  And freedom come at length?

Like dew on drooping blossoms,
  Like breath from holy place,
Laden with health and healing
  Come Thy deep words of grace:
'Thy strength is all in leaning,
  On One who fights for thee;
Thine is the helpless clinging,
  And Mine the victory."

NOT KNOWING.

I KNOW not what will befall me! God hangs a
mist o'er my eyes;
And o'er each step of my onward path He makes
new scenes to rise,
And every joy He sends me comes as a sweet and
glad surprise.

I see not a step before me, as I tread the days of
the year,
But the past is still in God's keeping, the future
His mercy shall clear,
And what looks dark in the distance, may brighten
as I draw near.

For perhaps the dreadful future has less bitterness
than I think;
The Lord may sweeten the water before I stoop to
drink.
Or, if Marah must be Marah, He will stand beside
its brink.

It may be there is waiting for the coming of my
feet
Some gift of such rare blessedness, some joy so
strangely sweet,
That my lips can only tremble with the thanks I
cannot speak.

O restful, blissful ignorance! 'Tis blessed not to know;
It keeps me quiet in those arms which will not let me go,
And hushes my soul to rest on the bosom which loves me so.

So I go on not knowing. I would not if I might;
I would rather walk in the dark with God, than go alone in the light,
I would rather walk with Him by faith, than walk alone by sight.

My heart shrinks back from trials which the future may disclose,
Yet I never had a sorrow but what the dear Lord chose;
So I send the coming tears back, with the whispered word, "He knows."

MY APPOINTED TIME.

I THOUGHT me near the pearly gate,
I thought I heard the Master call;
But I was wrong, and I must wait:
Not yet! I have not suffered all.

I thought I heard the angel's song,
That breaks like some eternal sea;

I thought I saw the countless throng
  Bending to God the rev'rent knee.

I thought I knew the sainted face
  Of many here whom I had known;
But glorified with some new grace,
  And into Jesus' likeness grown.

And, oh, I thought the kingly One,
  My soul delights its Lord to call,
Rose on my being like a sun;
  And like a sun outshone them all

But I was wrong; I am not ripe
  To enter on my endless rest:
Where God's own hand all tears shall wipe,
  And soothe each heavy-laden breast.

I have a will, yet, of my own:
  The Lord has work for me to do;
All earthly things I've not outgrown,
  Nor wholly put on all things new.

My time appointed I will wait,
  Until my last great change shall come;
Then He will open wide the Gate,
  And, satisfied, I shall go home.

LET ME FIND THEE

BEHOLD me here, in grief draw near,
  Pleading at Thy throne, O King!
To Thee each tear, each trembling fear,
  Jesus, Son of Man! I bring.
Let me find Thee—let me find Thee—
  Me, a vile and worthless thing!

Look down in love, and from above,
  With Thy Spirit satisfy;
Thou hast sought me, Thou hast bought me,
  And Thy purchase, Lord, am I.
Let me find Thee—let me find Thee,
  Here on earth, and then on high!

No other prayer to Thee I bear,
  O my Lord, but only this:
To share Thy grace, to see Thy face,
  And to know Thy people's bliss.
Let me find Thee—let me find Thee—
  Thee to find is blessedness!

Hear the broken, scarcely spoken
  Utterance of my heart to Thee;
All the crying, all the sighing,
  Of Thy child accepted be.
Let me find Thee—let me find Thee;
  Thus my soul longs vehemently!

Worldly pleasures, earthly treasures,
  Joys and honors, will not stay:
They often pain, and, oh! how vain,
  Looking to eternity!
Let me find Thee—let me find Thee—
  Find Thee, O my God, this day!

ENDURANCE.

HOW much the heart may bear, and yet not break!
  How much the flesh may suffer, and not die!
I question much if any pain or ache
  Of soul or body brings our end more nigh.
Death chooses his own time; till that is worn,
  All evils may be borne.

We shrink and shudder at the surgeon's knife;
  Each nerve recoiling from the cruel steel,
Whose edge seems searching for the quivering life
  Yet to our sense the bitter pangs reveal
That still, although the trembling flesh be torn,
  This, also can be borne.

We see a sorrow rising in our way,
  And try to flee from the approaching ill.
We seek some small escape—we weep and pray—
  But when the blow falls, then our hearts are still,
Not that the pain is of its sharpness shorn,
  But that it can be borne.

We wind our life about another life—
  We hold it closer, dearer than our own—
Anon it faints and falls in deadly strife,
  Leaving us stunned, and stricken, and alone;
But ah! we do not die with those who mourn—
        This, also, can be borne.

Behold, we live through all things—famine, thirst,
  Bereavement, pain! all grief and misery,
All woe and sorrow; life inflicts its worst
  On soul and body— but we cannot die,
Though we be sick, and tired, and faint, and worn;
        Lo! all things can be borne.

READY FOR ALL!

"READY, O Master!" with eager lip
    We cried when the day was new;
"And whatsoever Thy high commands,
Thy servants are waiting with willing hands,
    Prepared both to dare and to do!"

"Ready, O Master!"—No answer came,
    As we waited in weariness long:
Had He scorned the hands that were fain to bear
Their part in the burden—fain to share
    In the battle, the triumph, the song?

"Ready, O Master!" we cried once more,
As the long, long hours went by:
"Tell us Thy will! Is it woe or shame;
We will bear them both, for Thy blessed name,
For Thy name we would gladly die."

Softly the answer came—"O child!
Not such is My will for thee,
But only to stand in thy quiet lot,
Doing its duties and questioning not
What the wherefore or end may be."

O Infinite love, that has ordered thus!
Yet oft it more wearisome seems
Patiently thus to be serving here,
Than to carry the banner and sword and spear,
And fight in the fields of our dreams.

Patience! O questioning, wavering heart!
Good cheer and glad courage be thine!
The cup of cold water bestowed in His name,
Is sweeter than sacrifice, fairer than fame,
And the service itself is divine!

I WOULD HAVE GONE.

I WOULD have gone, God bade me stay,
I would have worked, God bade me rest;
He broke my will from day to day;
He read my yearnings unexpressed,
And said them nay.

Now I would stay, God bids me go,
Now I would rest, God bids me work;
He breaks my heart, tossed too and fro;
My soul is wrung with doubts that lurk
And vex it so.

I go, Lord, where Thou sendest me!
Day after day, I plod and moil,
But Christ, my Lord, when will it be
That I may let alone my toil,
And rest with Thee?

SUBMISSION.

GOD'S right-hand angel bright and calm—
Christ's strengthener in the agony—
Teach *us* the meaning of that psalm
Of fullness only known by thee:
"Thy will be done!" We sit alone,
And grief within our heart grows strong
With passionate moaning, 'till thou come,
And turn it tc a song.

Come when the days go heavily,
Weighed down with burdens hard to bear;
When joy and hope fail utterly,
And leave us fronted by despair.
Come not with flattering earthly light—

But with those clear grand eyes that see
Beyond the dark, beyond the bright,
Straight toward Eternity.

Teach us to work when work seems vain,
This is half victory over fate—
To match ourselves against our pain;
The rest is done when we can wait.
Unseal our eyes to see how rife
With bloom this thorny path may be;
And how it leads to heights of life
Which only thou canst see.

Content thee—so the angel saith—
Thy minor makes the triumph strain
Sound sweeter on celestial breath—
And God has use for all thy pain.
His joy thy struggling soul may reach;
From the strong slain comes sweetness still,
And God lets suffering only teach,
Some best revealings of His will.

Then strike within our hearts the key!
Though only sorrow's note it give,
Yet fit us for Thy Harmony,
And teach us how to live!

O patient watcher over all!
If broken lives may best complete
Thy circle, let our fragments fall
An offering at Thy feet.

'TWILL NOT BE LONG.

'TWILL not be long—this wearying commotion
  That marks its passage in the human breast
And, like the billows on the heaving ocean,
  That ever rock the cradle of unrest,
Will soon subside; the happy time is nearing,
  When bliss, not pain, shall have its rich increase,
E'en unto Thee the dove may now be steering
  With gracious message. Wait, and hold thy peace;
'Twill not be long!

The lamps go out; the stars give up their shining;
  The world is lost in darkness for awhile;
And foolish hearts give way to sad repining,
  And feel as though they ne'er again could smile.
Why murmur thus, the needful lesson scorning?
  Oh, read thy teacher and His word aright!
The world would have no greeting for the morning
  If 'twere not for the darkness of the night;
'Twill not be long!

'Twill not be long; the strife will soon be ended;
  The doubts, the fears, the agony, the pain,
Will seem but as the clouds that low descended
  To yield their pleasure to the parched plain.
The times of weakness and of sore temptations,
  Of bitter grief and agonizing cry;

These earthly cares and ceaseless tribulations
  Will bring a blissful harvest by-and-by—
          'Twill not be long!

'Twill not be long; the eye of faith discerning,
  The wondrous glory that shall be revealed,
Instructs the soul, that every day is learning
  The better wisdom which the world concealed.
And soon, aye, soon, there'll be an end of teaching,
  When mortal vision finds immortal sight,
And her true place the soul in gladness reaching,
  Beholds the glory of the Infinite.
          'Twill not be long!

"'Twill not be long! the heart goes on repeating;
  It is the burden of the mourner's song;
The work of grace in us he is completing,
  Who thus assures us—"It will not be long."
His rod and staff our fainting steps sustaining,
  Our hope and comfort every day will be;
And we may bear our cross as uncomplaining
  As He who leads us unto Calvary;
          'Twill not be long!

THE NOBLE ARMY OF MARTYRS PRAISE THEE.

NOT they alone who from the bitter strife
 Came forth victorious, yielding willingly
That which they deem most precious, even life,
 Content to suffer all things, Christ, for Thee;
Not they alone whose feet so firmly trod
 The pathway ending in rack, sword and flame,
Foreseeing death, yet faithful to their Lord,
 Enduring for His sake the pain and shame.
Not they alone have won the martyr's palm,
Not only from their lips proceeds the eternal psalm.

For earth hath martyrs now, a saintly throng,
 Each day unnoticed do we pass them by;
'Mid busy crowds they calmly move along,
 Bearing a hidden cross, how patiently!
Not theirs the sudden anguish, swift and keen,
 Their hearts are worn and wasted with small cares.
With daily griefs and thrusts from foes unseen,
 Troubles and trials that take them unawares;
Theirs is a lingering, silent martyrdom,
They weep through weary years, and long for rest
  to come.

They weep, but murmur not; it is God's will,
 And they have learned to bend their own to His,

Simply enduring, knowing that each ill
  Is but the herald of some future bliss;
Striving and suffering, yet so silently
  They know it least who seem to know them best,
Faithful and true through long adversity,
  They work and wait until God gives them rest;
These surely share with those of bygone days,
The palm-branch and the crown, and swell their
    song of praise.

BE STILL, AND KNOW THAT I AM GOD.

BE still, my child!
  I trod this way before;
My hand shall guide thee thro' the wild,
  Ask nothing more.

Be still, my child!
  I love thee first and last,
On Me, thy Saviour meek and mild,
  Thy sorrows cast.

Be still, my child!
  Leave all thy joys and fears,
I know thy hopes and longings wild,
  I see thy tears.

Be still, my child!
  My hand shall make the whole;

From every sin that hath defiled,
  Shall cleanse thy soul.

Be still, my child!
  And thou shalt feel My grace;
Come with a spirit meek and mild
  Before My face.

Be still, my child!
  And I will give thee peace;
When once My face on thee hath smiled,
  Thy woes shall cease.

Be still, my child!
  Until I call thee Home,
Then from thy wandering in the wild,
  Arise, and come!

JESUS, SAVIOUR, PILOT ME.

JESUS, Saviour, pilot me
  Over life's tempestuous sea:
Unknown waves before me roll,
Hiding rock and treacherous shoal;
Chart and compass came from Thee:
Jesus, Saviour, pilot me.

When the Apostles' fragile bark
Struggled with the billows dark,

On the stormy Galilee,
Thou didst walk upon the sea;
And when they beheld Thy form,
Safe they glided through the storm.

Though the sea be smooth and bright,
Sparkling with the stars of night,
And my ship's path be ablaze
With the light of halcyon days,
Still I know my need of Thee;
Jesus, Saviour, pilot me!

When the darkling heavens frown,
And the wrathful winds come down,
And the fierce waves, tossed on high,
Lash themselves against the sky,
Jesus, Saviour, pilot me
Over life's tempestuous sea.

As a mother stills her child
Thou canst hush the ocean wild;
Boisterous waves obey Thy will
When Thou sayest to them, "Be still."
Wondrous Sovereign of the sea,
Jesus, Saviour, pilot me.

When at last I near the shore,
And the fearful breakers roar
'Twixt me and the peaceful rest,

Then, while leaning on Thy breast,
May I hear Thee say to me,
'*Fear not, I will pilot thee!*'"

"DRAW NIGH TO GOD, AND HE WILL DRAW NIGH TO YOU."

WEARY and faint
Our garments stained with sin and soiled with tears—
Not tears that fall like blessed summer rain,
But heavy drops of pain,
Wrung from the heart's deep passion and distress,
Wrung from the yearning of its tenderness—
Thus—with the guilt and grief of days and years
We do draw nigh.

Yes— we draw nigh!
We are not worthy, Lord, to seek Thy face—
Not worthy—for our need is all our plea—
Yet may we come to Thee—
Nor fear to bring our darkness to Thy light,
All pure and holy in Thy perfect sight,
Clad in the white robe of our Saviour's grace—
So we draw nigh.

Yes, we draw nigh—
To Thee, the Comforter, we come for peace,—
Thou knowest, Lord, our weakness and our fear,
And Thou wilt surely hear,—

Wilt hear the cry that from life's wild wide sea
Rises from hearts that only cling to Thee;—
One look, one word, can bid our anguish cease—
So we draw nigh.

Thou wilt draw nigh!
Father—it is no dream that Thou art near—
No dream that, in my sin and misery,
I may look up to Thee,—
May hide beneath the shadow of Thy wings,
From all the restlessness of outward things,
And from my own heart's self-accusing fear—
For Thou art nigh!

TO MYSELF.

LET nothing make thee sad or fretful,
Or too regretful,
Be still;
What God hath ordered must be right,
Then find in it thine own delight,
My will.

Why shouldst thou fill to-day with sorrow
About to-morrow,
My heart?
One watches all with care most true,
Doubt not that He will give thee, too,
Thy part.

Only be steadfast, never waver,
Nor seek earth's favor,
But rest:
Thou knowest what God wills must be,
For all His creatures, so for thee,
The best.

"THE LORD KNOWETH."

THE Lord knoweth where each flower groweth
That bloometh for Him 'midst these earthly fields.
Though men despise it, He will fondly prize it,
Welcome the offering that its fragrance yields.

The Lord knoweth when the rough wind bloweth
Upon the weary and the laden one;
With tender feeling for the suppliant kneeling,
He shields and strengthens till the storm is done.

The Lord knoweth when each hot tear floweth
From eyes of those who suffer while they pray.
He knows their sorrow, in the glad to-morrow
Will wipe in gentleness those drops away.

The Lord knoweth when each servant soweth
With heavy heart and seemingly in vain;
When, after sleeping, there will come the reaping,
Will grant glad harvests where they toiled in pain.

The Lord knoweth when the mourner goeth
  To weep her loneliness by cherished grave.
Unseen He speaketh to the heart that breaketh :
  "I can restore him, for 'tis I that save."

The Lord knoweth when the wand'rer throweth
  Some little incense on His altar-fire ;
Sees his contrition, welcomes his petition,
  Tells his repentance to the heavenly choir.

The Lord knoweth when the slow pulse showeth
  That we are drawing near to Jordan's strand
When our heart faileth, then His strength availeth,
  And brings us safely to the better land.

The Lord knoweth ! If your faint heart troweth
  It is uncared for by its God above,
Oh ! doubt no longer, but in this be stronger :
  He knoweth all things, and His name is Love.

GUESTS OF THE HEART.

SOFT falls through the gathering twilight
  The rain from the dripping eaves,
And stirs with a tremulous rustle
  The dead and the dying leaves ;
While afar, in the midst of the shadows,
  I hear the sweet voices of bells,
Come borne on the wind of the Autumn
  That fitfully rises and swells.

They call and they answer each other,
 They answer and mingle again,
As the deep and the shrill in an anthem
 Make harmony still in their strain
As the voices of sentinels mingle
 In mountainous regions of snow,
Till from hill-top to hill-top a chorus
 Floats down to the valleys below.

The shadows, the fire-light of even,
 The sound of the rain's distant chime,
Come bringing, with rain softly dropping,
 Sweet thoughts of a shadowy time;
The slumberous sense of seclusion,
 From storm and intruders aloof,
We feel when we hear in the midnight
 The patter of rain on the roof.

When the spirit goes forth in its yearnings
 To take all its wanderers home;
Or, afar in the regions of fancy,
 Delights on swift pinions to roam,
I quietly sit by the fire-light—
 The fire-light so bright and so warm—
For I know that those only who love me
 Will seek me through shadow and storm.

But should they be absent this evening,
 Should even the household depart,
Deserted, I should not be lonely,
 There still would be guests in my heart.

The faces of friends that I cherish,
  The smile, and the glance, and the tone,
Will haunt me wherever I wander,
  And thus I am never alone.

With those who have left far behind them
  The joys and the sorrows of time—
Who sing the sweet songs of the angels
  In a purer and holier clime!
Then darkly, O evening of Autumn,
  Your rain and your shadows may fall:
My loved and my lost ones you bring me—
  My heart holds a feast with them all.

THE JOYFUL CALL.

OH, wayward soul,
  Dost thou not see the beckoning hand?
Dost thou not hear the blest command,
      The Saviour's call?
    He bids thee now rejoice.
    Must His beseeching voice
      On deaf ears fall?

      Oh, fainting heart,
Torn by so many doubts and fears,
Struggling midst many sighs and tears
      In anguish sore,
    Oh, raise thy tear-dimmed eyes
    Upward, above the skies,
      Forever more.

Arise and go,
The blessed Lord hath need of thee.
Hear even now His tender plea:
Be of good cheer.
He'll be thy dearest friend,
Keep thee unto the end;
Be ever near.

Take up thy cross,
Then shalt thou find the burden light,
The path made straight, the way all bright,
Thy warfare cease.
So shalt thou win thy crown,
At last thy life lay down
In perfect peace.

A little while
To toil below for His dear sake,
Then sweetly sleep in Him and wake
To thy reward!
Oh, holy, happy rest!
To be forever blest
In Christ thy Lord.

THE TRUST OF THE TRIED.

TO God's all-gracious heart and mind
My heart and mind I yield;
In seeming loss my gain I find,
In death, life stands revealed.

I am His own whose glorious throne
  In highest heaven is set;
Beneath His stroke or sorrow's yoke
  His heart upholds me yet.

There is but one thing cannot fail,
  That is my Father's love;
A sea of troubles may assail
  My soul,—'tis but to prove
And train my mind, by warnings kind,
  To love the good through pain;
When firm I stand, full soon His hand
  Can raise me up again.

Yet oft we think, is aught withdrawn
  That flesh and blood desire,
Our joy is lost, o'ercast our dawn,
  And faith and courage tire;
With toil and care our hearts we wear,
  O'er our lost hope we brood;
Nor think that all that doth befall
  Is meant to work our good.

But when God rules it must be so,
  It must bring joy again;
What now we deem but cross and woe
  Shall turn to comfort then.
Have patience still, His gracious will
  Through thickest cloud shall gleam;
Then torturing fears, and hopeless tears,
  Shall vanish like a dream.

The field can never bear its fruits,
  Save winter storm and freeze;
Man's goodness withers at its roots
  In days of constant ease;
The bitter draught of aloes quaffed,
  Health tints the cheeks once more;
So to our heart can sorrow's smart
  New energy restore.

Then, O my God, with joy I cast
  My load of care on Thee;
Take me, and while this life shall last
  Do as Thou wilt with me.
Send weal or woe, as Thou shalt know
  Will teach me their true worth,
And fit me best to stand their test,
  And show Thy glory forth.

If happy sunshine be Thy gift,
  With joy I take it, Lord;
If o'er dark stormy seas I drift,
  I hear Thy guiding word;
If lengthened life, with blessings rife,
  Before my feet be spread,
So Thou my guide wilt still abide,
  With joy that path I tread.

But must I walk the vale of death
  Through sad and sunless ways?
I pass along in quiet faith,
  Thy glance my fear allays;

Through the dark land my Shepherd's hand
  Leads to an end so bright,
That I shall there with praise declare,
  That all God's ways are right!

GONE.

LIST to the midnight lone!
  The church clock speaketh with a solemn tone—
    Doth it no more than tell the time?
    Hark! from that belfry gray,
In each deep-booming chime, which, slow and clear
Beats like a measured bell upon my ear,
    A stern voice seems to say:
        Gone—gone;
    The hour is gone—the day is gone;
        Pray!

The air is hushed again,
But the darkness woos to sleep in vain.
    O Soul! we have slept too long.
    Yes, dreamed the morn away
In visions false, and feverish unrest,
Wasting the work-time God hath given and blest.
    Conscience grows pale to see
    How, like a haunting face,
My youth stares at me out of gloom profound:
With rayless eyes, black as the darkness round,

And waiting lips which say:
Gone—gone;
The morn is gone—the morn is gone;
Pray!

Woe for the wasted years
Born bright with smiles, but buried with sad tears,
Their tombs have been prepared
By Time, that gravesman gray;
Soul, we may weep to count each stone,
And read the epitaph engraved thereon
By that stern carver's hand.
Yet weep not long, for Hope,
Steadfast and calm, beside each headstone stands
Gazing on Time, with upward-pointing hands.
Take we this happy sign,
Up! let us work and pray.

Thou in whose sight the hoary ages fly
Swift as a summer's noon, yet whose stern eye
Doth note each moment lost,
So let me live, that not one hour misspent
May rise in judgment on me, penitent,
But, till the sunset, Lord,
So in Thy vineyard toil,
That every hour a priceless gem may be,
To crown the blind brows of Eternity.

ROCK OF AGES.

"ROCK of Ages, cleft for me"—
Thoughtlessly the maiden sung,
Fell the words unconsciously,
From her girlish, gleeful tongue;
Sang as little children sing;
Sang as sing the birds in June;
Fell the words like light leaves down
On the current of the tune—
"Rock of Ages, cleft for me,
Let me hide myself in Thee."

"Let me hide myself in Thee,"
Felt her soul no need to hide:
Sweet the song as song could be—
And she had no thought beside;
All the words unheedingly
Fell from lips untouched by care,
Dreaming not they each might be
On some other lips a prayer—
"Rock of Ages, cleft for me,
Let me hide myself in Thee."

"Rock of Ages, cleft for me"—
'Twas a woman sung them now,
Pleadingly and prayerfully;
Every word her heart did know.
Rose the song as storm-tossed bird
Beats with weary wing the air,

Every note with sorrow stirred—
  Every syllable a prayer—
"Rock of Ages, cleft for me,
  Let me hide myself in Thee."

"Rock of Ages, cleft for me"—
  Lips grown aged sung the hymn
Trustingly and tenderly—
  Voice grown weak and eyes grown dim.
"Let me hide myself in Thee"—
  Trembling though the voice and low,
Ran the sweet strain peacefully,
  Like a river in its flow.
Sung as only they can sing,
  Who behold the promised rest—
"Rock of Ages cleft for me,
  Let me hide myself in Thee."

"Rock of Ages, cleft for me"—
  Sung above a coffin lid;
Underneath, all restfully,
  All life's joys and sorrows hid.
Never more, O storm-tossed soul,
  Never more from wind or tide,
Never more from billow's roll,
  Wilt thou need thyself to hide.
Could the sightless, sunken eyes,
  Closed beneath the soft gray hair,

Could the mute and stiffened lips
  Move again in pleading prayer,
Still, aye, still, the words would be,
"Let me hide myself in Thee."

"UNTIL HE COME."

"TILL He come!"—oh, let the words
  Linger on the trembling chords;
Let the little while between,
In their golden light be seen;
Let us think how heaven and home
Lie beyond that "Till He come."

When the weary ones we love
Enter on their rest above,
Seems the earth so poor and vast,
All our life-joy overcast?
Hush! be every murmur dumb;
It is only "Till He come."

Clouds and conflicts round us press;
Would we have one sorrow less?
All the sharpness of the cross,
All that tells the world is loss,
Death and darkness and the tomb
Only whisper, "Till He come."

See, the feast of love is spread!
Drink the wine and break the bread;
Sweet memorials!—till the Lord
Call us round His heavenly board;
Some from earth, from glory some,
Severed only—till He come.

PRAYING.

CLOSE, close, beloved mine,
Around my heart entwine,
In Love's strong clasping, as I hold thee, so.
Above the sky that leans
Over these deathful scenes,
To Him, the Eternal Life and Love, we go.

Back from His awful light,
Back from consuming sight,
Of glory infinite, His cherubim
Stand reverently veiled.
Before His splendor paled,
All majesty, all brightness waneth dim.

Yet see, anear His feet,
White-robed, and chanting sweet
Their song of love, His ransomed myriads bow.
For them, on cruel rood,
Did Jesus give His blood:
Nearest of all in Heaven, they worship now.

Think! is our yearning love
Caught from His heart above?
Then haste we, blend our voices with that choir.
In noblest strains they pour;
We vie with them, and soar
Until our souls are with His love on fire.

Alas! not rapturous strain,
Unsaddened now with pain,
Befits us, until Life's fleet changes cease.
Our sinning we confess,
Our needs we meekly press,
And crave the seal-kiss of His hallowed peace.

O Merciful! we pray,
Absolve our guilt away;
Give victory against temptation still;
With cheerful grace endue
These hearts that, weeping, sue
Too oft for respite from Thy blessed will.

In us Thy will be done.
Touch Thou the spirit tone
That brings our life with Thine in sweet accord
In sacred oneness bound,
Circled by love profound,
Thy Love—enfold us to Thy bosom, Lord.

INDEX TO SUBJECTS.

INDEX TO FIRST LINES.

www.ingramcontent.com/pod-product-compliance
Lightning Source LLC
LaVergne TN
LVHW010224110826
845151LV00004B/1180

9781425526702